STO

1-22-75

1-22-75

G.L.S.
SHACKLE

•

KEYNESIAN
KALEIDICS

•

The evolution of a
general political
economy

•

EDINBURGH
UNIVERSITY
PRESS

•

© 1974 G. L. S. Shackle
Edinburgh University Press
22 George Square, Edinburgh
ISBN 0 85224 260 3
North America
Aldine Publishing Company
529 South Wabash Avenue, Chicago
Library of Congress
Catalog Card Number 73-91497
Printed in Great Britain

Preface

Keynes suggested in a number of passages that his essential theory of money, employment, general output and the price-level could be very briefly stated. By contrast, the form his work took was an evolution from the long but confident and seductive *Treatise on Money*, through the complex, many-faced and difficult *General Theory*, to the apocalyptic article, called 'The General Theory of Employment', in which he destroyed in one sentence the basic assumption of conventional economics, that business can and does proceed by reason and calculation based on sufficient data. That basis is absent, he said in effect, *in the nature of things*. In hewing his way to that conclusion, he sometimes pressed into service conceptual tools quite alien to his purpose and to each other. The bold encapsulation achieved by the Fundamental Equations of the *Treatise* was abandoned in the *General Theory* in favour of ostensible appeals to 'equilibrium'. Between the *Treatise* and the *General Theory* he went from good methods to bad, from clarity to obscurity, yet filled the great gap in the argument of the *Treatise* by bringing in the Inducement to Invest. In the two books taken together, which are all one book, there is no consistent method but there is brilliant improvisation. Critics, however, have made little complaint about method, perhaps because they do not acknowledge the *meaning* as a subversion of the established appeal to rationality.

The invitation from the University of Wales, which afforded the occasion for developing this theme in five lectures delivered in Cardiff and Swansea during the autumn term of 1972, gave me an unforgettable experience of warmth, friendship and generosity. I wish in especial to thank Professor Edward

Nevin, Professor Brinley Thomas and Professor Sir Bryan Hopkin for their endless kindness.

G. L. S. Shackle, 26 *July* 1973

NOTE
Page references to the *Treatise on Money* refer to the Collected Works edition. Page references to the *Treatise on Probability* refer to the original edition. The pagination of the first edition of the *General Theory* has been preserved in the Collected Works edition.

Contents

to Brinley Thomas

1. Money and Employment

Keynes wrote in succession *A Treatise on Money* [1] and *The General Theory of Employment, Interest and Money*. [2] The latter was written in the years immediately following the publication in 1930 of the former, because Keynes thought, when he had written the *Treatise*, that he 'could do it better and much shorter if [he] were to start over again'. The two books, then, are the same book. Yet they are ostensibly different in many, seemingly important, respects. How do they come to have unity, in some sense, in theme and purpose, and yet use such different apparatus? And why (this is even more interesting for the theoretician) does *money* appear in the title of both books?

The *Treatise* is *about* money. Its purpose is to examine the nature and effects of money, and, in particular, to study that question which value theory leaves aside, namely, what is the source and mechanism of changes in the general level of money prices of goods. The theory of value explains their prices in terms of each other. It does not explain their prices in terms of something whose only ultimate use is to be got rid of in exchange for something useful in itself.

'When I began to write my *Treatise on Money* (Keynes says in the Preface to the *General Theory*) I was still moving along the traditional lines of regarding the influence of money as something so to speak separate from the general theory of supply and demand. When I finished it, I had made some progress towards pushing monetary theory back to becoming a theory of output as a whole.'

In the *Treatise*, the object of study is money itself, whatever

that word may be found to mean. Since money depends for its
significance, in the last analysis, on the act of exchanging it for
the means of sustaining and enjoying life, a lot of the significance of money is presumably to be found in the ratios of exchange of money for goods; in the sources, mechanisms and
consequences of changes in those ratios; and in the principles
by which those changes can be manipulated and the question
of what ends such manipulation ought to serve. In the *Theory*,
Keynes had been driven by the dramatic and disastrous history
of those times, the early 1930s, to single out one particular
class of the consequences of money, namely, its role and responsibility in engendering massive general unemployment.
But he has gone further. For now the object of study has
changed. It is output as a whole and the question what governs
and affects its size, and thus governs the level of employment.
In answering the question about general output and about
employment, money has an essential and indispensable part to
play, so vital a part that we can still deem the *General Theory*
to be a theory of money. To say this is to say that massive general unemployment is a monetary phenomenon. But this does
not mean that it is a phenomenon of that hydraulic money discussed in the Quantity Theory's various versions and elabora-
tions. It does not mean, even, that the famous IS–LM curves
will serve as a vessel for its essence. For though, as Sir John
Hicks has told us at a seminar in his honour in the summer of
1972, Keynes in a letter to Sir John gave his approval to these
curves, they conform to only one of the two faces of Keynes's
work which we shall seek to distinguish. According to one of
those faces, the effects of money are amenable to orderly dis-
section; according to the other, we must conclude that money
is what unbuckles the harness and allows the horses to gallop
off into the wild.

But money is a manifestation or aspect or recourse of something in our experience which rises from the very roots of conscious being, namely, the fact that our existence consists in
continually finding out what is happening. Consciousness is
finding out. If there is always something to find out, it follows

that we do not yet know everything, that we do not ever know everything. The things we do not, at any moment, know are the whole future near and remote, mundane and trivial or momentous. Of course our short-term guesswork often comes out right. Experience is some use. You switch on the engine of your car and it starts, you strike a match and it produces a flame. Besides, there is the seemingly recurrent temporal frame of Nature, the succession of night and day and of the seasons. There is some degree of assurance concerning the sequel to particular states of affairs and particular manipulations, which makes daily life practicable. But, we do not *know*, if knowing consists in the possession of demonstrable certainty. When we consider such things as who will win the Derby or the election, or where the *Financial Times* index of Stock Exchange prices will be in six months' time, or what will be the outcome if I embark my fortune in starting a business, it is difficult to claim anything approaching demonstrable certainty. To so do would be to invite the mockery of Fate. Yet what has economic theory done? It has constructed the theory of value on the basis of a clear-cut, simple-sounding assumption, namely, that men pursue their interests by applying reason to their circumstances. How simple, if only we can dispose of the question how they know what their circumstances are.

The theory of value has to build for itself a world where that problem is solvable. If the future cannot be known, there must be no future. Value-theory has to start by abolishing the future and declaring itself to be concerned only with a world encompassed in a single moment. By doing this, however, it disposes of another problem. In its single-moment world, the theory of value has only to ascribe to each individual a complete and perfect knowledge of his relevant circumstances of that unique moment. But even those circumstances include, for each person, the particular action which is going to be chosen and performed in that moment by each other person. How can *each* person *choose* his action (for example, the quantity of goods of some kind which he will exchange) in knowledge of what each of the others is choosing? It can be done, in effect. It can be done by pooling of statements of conditional intentions and the finding of a general solution or General Equilibrium which shall prescribe for each person, as the action to be taken by him, the very action he would prefer, given that each other person is committed to perform the particular action prescribed for him. It is such a solution which it is the peculiar, characteristic and especial duty of the re-contract market (in Edgeworth's language) or the *tâtonnements* market (in Walras's language) to find.

In the momentary world of value theory, what would be the need or use of money? Who would want to exchange something useful in itself for something useless in itself? To exchange some consumable or usable good for money, a token good, is only one half of a complete exchange of good for good. The other half waits to be performed. But would money, perhaps, make it easier to find the man who has what you want and wants what you have? Not at all. That function is performed implicitly as part of the nature of the General Equilibrium. General Equilibrium, the Theory of Value, has no possible use for money. If there is no tomorrow, there is no point in keeping spending-power for tomorrow. But there would not be in any case, if we could know precisely and for certain what we were going to need tomorrow. Money is only of use in a world where things are *not* certain, are *not* completely known or even knowable, where the fantasy that all knowledge can be had *at a cost* does not prevail.

Keynes did not, of course, go into all this. He took it for granted that he was writing about a world which does use money, and which finds the need to do so in the Scheme of Things itself, where we assume that day will follow day and year will follow year, and where this assumption bears on what we do and what we refrain from doing *to-day*.

What we refrain from doing to-day is to use up and destroy the equivalent of every pennyworth of to-day's production; to-day's *value added*. If we were all subsistence farmers, Robinson Crusoes each entirely self-sufficient, the excess of to-day's value-added over to-day's using-up would necessarily add itself to stock in the form of material objects, stock-piles of foods, fuel, clothing and so on, or in the form of flocks and herds, or in the form perhaps of newly-made tools. It would be in the form of specific, specialized products each having natural and technological characteristics, adapted to some tasks, applications and purposes, perhaps of a wide ultimate diversity, but *bounded* so long as those purposes are confined to a definite time-interval stretching forward from 'to-day', confined to a definite horizon, and confined also to a given state of technological knowledge. But we are not self-sufficient Robinson Crusoes. We can accept our income, initially, in the form of money, and we can stock-pile our provision for the future in the form of money. Or can we?

What would be the use of money, in a world where there were not any goods? Even if each one of us is free to save money, that act of saving will only make sense if the money saved out of to-day's or this week's money income represents and corresponds to some real value added, some technological transformation of one outfit of materials and tools into a some-what different one, a more useful, more valuable one. So the act of providing for the future, of stock-piling wealth, of im-proving our material armour against years to come, of *pro-ducing additional means of production*, must involve, and essentially consist in, the bringing into existence of specific *forms*; of specific kinds of stuff; of tools, engines, plant and systems, all of them having *specific* technological design. But who knows whether, when the time comes to apply them, they will turn out to be of the right design, of the best design, of an unsuperseded, still relatively efficient design, who knows whether they will be what the market of that day desires? Someone has got to answer that unanswerable question. How do you answer the unanswerable? By conjecture, by *committed* conjecture, by gambling on your guess.

When the investment-goods, which correspond to the saved income, are produced, they have to belong to someone. Some-one must assume the responsibility, must bear the risk, must

embark part of his fortune in this ownership. Those who
merely save *money* do not do so.

There are thus two relationships to the business of improving and augmenting the society's equipment, its designed,
oriented, purposeful stock-pile of wealth. That improvement
and augmentation is *permitted* to occur without a general rise
of prices by those members of the society who, being suppliers
of productive services, and, correspondingly, income-disposers,
do not elect to consume the whole of their annual or weekly
produce. The improvement and augmentation is actually designed in detail, and performed, by some of those composite
characters (encompassing the roles of managers, technologists,
shareholders) whom we are calling business men or enterprisers or employers. These business men are the payers of the
incomes, to their employees and to themselves, which measure
and represent the production of goods in general. Thus, in
effect, the equipment, the making of which is part of to-day's
or this week's total value added, part of this week's total production, is in one sense *owned*, and in another sense *borrowed
from the society as a whole*, by the business men. It is owned
by the business men in the sense that, if the equipment or any
items of it were to turn out to be worthless, the loss would be
theirs. It is borrowed, in the sense that the members of society
all taken together, including the business men, have refrained
from consuming as much as they might, thus leaving part of
the product to be stockpiled. Now on the face of it, it would
not be surprising if the enterprisers, those who invest in equipment, and the savers, those who allow equipment to be produced although they themselves are thus debarred from consuming part of their product, should have different ideas about
the proportions in which that product should consist of consumables and investment goods. For the savers do not undertake
the risks of ownership of highly specific, complex, invention-
vulnerable equipment. They save *money*, which can always be
spent on *something*.

This idea can be seen in a highly concentrated form if we
consider the dual personality of the business man himself. He

is both employer and supplier of productive services, he is both payer and recipient of income. As recipient of income he may wish to save a large proportion, as employer he may be loth to be saddled with a great increment of equipment whose value is sensitive to technological, fashionable and other unpredictable market influence. Yet if he refuses so to saddle himself, the general output will be that much smaller, employment will be less.

By *involuntary* unemployment it is natural to mean unemployment which no action of the unemployed themselves can cure. But can there be such a thing? Why should not any person, who has valuable productive services to offer, be able to get them accepted, that is, get himself and his possessions employed, by offering them for less than the value they have for an employer? Let us examine the terms of this question.

What is the value of productive services to an employer? And before we can answer that we must decide, *in terms of what* is that value to be measured? Two natural means of measurement suggest themselves : the product itself, linked in quantity to the quantities of the productive services by a technological production-function ; and the price which the product will fetch in the market. And already we have taken one more step into the deeps of meaning. For what business have we to suppose that the employer knows, when he engages labour, what price per unit the product will fetch? Let us then at first measure the value of productive services in terms of product. The value of those services to an employer, the value to him of any precise quantity of any specific service, applied in specific circumstances, is the difference this application will make to the amount of his weekly, *et cetera*, production. If he can pay his work people in product, an employer can afford, as we all know, to pay them at the rate of their marginal product. But there is still a question. By what right does he call himself an employer, let alone an *enterpriser*, if he compels his collaborators to share with him the immediate risks of enterprise? To pay his people in product is to make them his partners, it is to make each of them a merchant in Cantillon's meaning, a man who buys goods at a known price in order to sell them, later on, at a price which now he cannot know. We are face to face again with the indissoluble link between money and uncertainty, between money and un-knowledge.

Suppliers of productive services who are willing to be paid in product are shareholders in the enterprise. The reason why they can have no difficulty in getting themselves employed is that they are willing to employ themselves. By confining our questions and our arguments to a part of the field from which money is excluded, we exclude the real questions and the real difficulties. By excluding money we assume away unemployment, because we thus assume away the question of knowledge, of how people can know what they need to know for certainty of successful conduct of their affairs. We are seeing already the unity of the elements of Keynes's title: *The General Theory of Employment, Interest and Money*. Money and employment do belong in the same skein of ideas.

Before we proceed, let us clear the path we have been following of a few questions. We have been talking of the amount of weekly production; and of differences of this amount. What is production? What is produced? Extra usefulness, extra power to satisfy needs or desires, is given to some pre-existing outfit of materials and tools. The physical or technological character of these things is changed in greater or less degree, and they emerge in a new form more suitable to human purpose. Coal or oil or natural gas is removed from the ground to where its energy can be released; crops are harvested, materials are fabricated and assembled, transported and retailed. In these ways *value is added* to the initial outfit. Value added is a direct measure of the production which has been done. We need not make any deduction for what has been 'used up'. That allowance is implicit in the meaning of valued *added*. Provided this value added can be measured, a man can be offered employment in some firm at a wage not greater than the difference his presence makes to that firm's weekly total of valued added. If he is willing to work for such a wage, he will find himself employed. If he is not willing to work for this wage, is he then *involuntarily* unemployed? Not within the definition we have proposed. The questions are, then, whether and how value added and its differences can be measured. But before we can answer this there is another question : *When* are they to be measured? Plainly they must be measured at the moment when the enterpriser's decision is being taken about how much employment to give, whether or not to engage a particular extra man. The measurement of value-added must be made *before value has been added*. It must be made *ex ante*. The employer is Cantillon's merchant, who signs contracts to obtain the means of production at known prices in order to sell, when it shall have been produced, a product whose price, when he makes these contracts, he does not know. How then can he know what an extra man's work will be worth to him? He cannot know, or he would have no claim to be called an enterpriser, and that is the point.

That point is given its full and overwhelming importance when the product is an investment good, a durable tool or system of productive facilities whose value in the present (and there is no other place for value to exist) depends on conjectures concerning distant future years. When value depends on expectations, on a skein of rival answers about the sequel to a contemplated act, the employer cannot *know* how big the difference is which an extra man would make to his value-added ; and thus this extra man's claim, to be employed because the wage he asks is less than that difference, loses its meaning and force.

This theme in this form is not to be found in Keynes's work. But it is an immediate consequence of that thread of thought which runs persistently through the *General Theory* though often concealed, the theme that economic action flows from expectation and is accordingly the creature of uncertainty, mutability and precarious faith. The task of the reader of that book is to disentangle that single, glittering thread from the skein of ancillary notions, arguments, suggestions and general supporting and disguising strands in which Keynes saw fit to wrap it, and from which he did not, until after the book was written, succeed in his own thought in freeing it.

Before he could start to explain the source and nature of *involuntary* unemployment, Keynes felt obliged to show that this notion is logically existent, that is, that it does not contain an internal self-contradiction. And in especial, he felt that he must overcome the value-theorist's instinctive, immediate and ostensibly fatal objection, namely, that any man can find employment at a wage not greater than his marginal product. It is to this preliminary task that Keynes addresses himself in the first substantive chapter of the *General Theory*, chapter 2. And he does so in a very odd way.

The attitude of the Theory of Value to money is that money does not matter. Money is a *numéraire*, a mathematically convenient economizer of words or other notation. It is permissible to speak in terms of money-prices, but these are a simplified expression of the notion of a set of mutually and comprehensively consistent exchange-ratios between all possible pairs of *goods useful in themselves*. Thus the Theory of Value does not concern itself with any distinction between money wages and real wages. Its theory of employment is that labour will be demanded up to the point where its marginal product is no greater than the wage, and supplied up to that point where the utility of the wage is no greater than the disutility of the marginal supply of labour. These two equations determine the two unknowns, the wage-rate and the level of employment. Thus employment is naturally, necessarily and always full. There cannot be any involuntary unemployment. Keynes saw his first task to be the breaking-out from this impasse. And his means of doing so was ready to the thoughts of a theoretician of money.

Changes in the level of money prices of goods bought by wage-earners, in relation to the level of money rates of wages, must affect the situation of employers and employed, and their conduct. If wage-goods, the things on which employed people spend their incomes, fall in price a little in relation to the money wage, this will make it a little less profitable for employers to produce wage goods for sale to employees, and will lead to some reduction in the numbers employed. At the same time it will make employment seem, at the margin, more desirable than before, and lead to an increase in the number of people desiring jobs. In two ways, therefore, it will increase the number of people who desire jobs and have not got them. But cannot these people lower the money-wage at which they, and through their competition, others also, offer their labour? Yes, but the effect will be to reduce the flow of money being offered for wage-goods, since the aggregate incomes of wage-earners will thus be reduced. If by this reduction the money-prices of wage-goods are reduced, the profitability of producing wage-goods may not be restored, and unemployment, *involuntary* unemployment, will remain. Thus Keynes, by an argument occupying fifteen out of the eighteen pages of chapter 2, prised open a chink in the armour of the 'classical' view that full employment is natural and guaranteed. Would the *General Theory* have been worth writing if this was all?

Chapter 2, having nearly spent itself on attaining the result that money illusion can weaken the force of the classical belief and theory of natural equilibrium in the employment market, suddenly abandons that line of thought and takes up something entirely fresh : the question whether and in what sense effective demand for goods in general is necessarily equal to their supply. Suddenly, in the last three pages of the chapter, a new question is asked and a new landscape revealed. In a remarkable paragraph of seventy words, Keynes sets out the heart of a theory of the non-identity, the quantitative separability, of saving and investment, and what is most remarkable and most tantalizing of all, he attains this result by recourse to an *ex ante* view of the quantities involved, by speaking, in fact, of these quantities as *decisions*. Could he but have carried through the *General Theory* on this track, what a vast difference would have been made to the penetrative power of his ideas into the minds of economists then, and still to-day, convinced that men's economic conduct is based on fully-informed rationality. This remarkable paragraph, unique in the *General Theory* in its grasp of the elusive essence, is as follows:

'They are fallaciously supposing that there is a nexus which unites decisions to abstain from present consumption with decisions to provide for future consumption; whereas the motives which determine the latter are not linked in any simple way with the motives which determine the former.' (p. 21)

There is no explicit recognition, here or elsewhere in the *General Theory*, nor even in those articles in the *Economic Journal*[3] for 1937 where Keynes engaged in the great debate with his critics, of the fact that quantities referring to the future are not in their nature and essence reducible to a *consistent table of accounts*. They are no more 'accountable' in this way than two plays about fictional characters are necessarily capable of being matched in plot and story. The future is each man's own imaginative figment, based on the particular suggestions which have come his way, the particular straws that the wind of events happens to have blown into his eyes, interpreted and pieced together in the light shed by his personal, unique individual history and experience. The notion that economic quantities, referring *ex ante* to some proper-named calendar interval such as October, 1972, are each unique and determinable and consistent with each other, is a notion derived from classical mechanics or from traditional book-keeping. It appears to be ineradicable. Even to-day it is considered good enough to extrapolate the past and call it the future.

No theory of general massive unemployment, of involuntary unemployment, could prevail which did not release the reasoning from the 'classical' conclusion that full employment is natural and self-guaranteeing. Full employment, the mutual determination of the wage-rate and the level of employment, is not even a conclusion of General Equilibrium so much as a part or aspect of its premisses. If knowledge is complete and perfect, if we are discussing a world from which un-knowledge of relevant things is excluded by the very design and basis of that world, then nothing can occur which can be called involuntary, save in the sense that such a world would be deterministic. Keynes begins his book by attempting this release, by confronting this logically prior question, *how can there be* involuntary unemployment? He devotes chapter 2 entirely to this plainly and insistently crucial matter. And his solution, until the last page or two of that chapter, is *money illusion*. Until those last pages, the task of destroying a theory which would make involuntary unemployment impossible is left to a supposed indifference on labour's part to a moderate rise of prices. Then, without warning, in section VI, there is a glimpse of something new and momentous. In a brief paragraph (lines 10–18 of page 21) Keynes seizes again, as he did in the *Treatise*, the idea that investment and saving can in some way be different from each other. But the nature and meaning of this mutual freedom eludes him. The idea that different people's conceptions of what will flow from their intended actions in the imagined circumstances of those actions can be infinitely various and incompatible, and that these conceptions can, and almost must, diverge widely and wildly from what, at the end of some interval, we shall be able to look back on, was not formulated by Keynes, in the *General Theory* or elsewhere, in any effective form to which his thought responded or which his mind exploited. Yet this idea would have provided him with a means of release immeasurably more powerful than money illusion.

Why is it that employers and employed, enterprisers who demand productive services and the suppliers of those services, cannot talk the same language, and arrive at an equilibrium where the marginal disutility of labour would be matched by the marginal utility of the wage, and where the marginal product of labour would make the wage just worth paying by the employers? They cannot do so, because the desired *real composition* of the wage is not the same for the two groups. For the employed or would-be employed, the desired incomes in real composition contain a relatively high proportion of accretions of wealth as compared with immediately consumable goods. For the enterprisers, such a high proportion can at times of especial uncertainty be undesired, because it is they, and not their employees, not their suppliers of productive services, who will be the actual owners, the potential loser-gainer-gamblers, of the newly produced equipment which must come into existence through the giving of a particular level of employment to people who insist on saving some of their income. The reason why *money* destroys the full-employment nexus is that it makes possible the divergent composition of the incomes that employing enterprisers are willing to pay and the incomes that suppliers of service are willing to receive. Keynes's chapter 2, at the very outset of his book, betrays the lack of the distinction of *ex ante* from *ex post*, a distinction as essential and indispensable as that of knowledge from ignorance, deed from idea, the possible, the conceived, the imagined, from the recorded and petrified fact.

Uncertainty, the notion of the skein of manifold and rival hypotheses, the plural answers entertained for some one question, is deeply involved in the nature of money. The relation of our need for a general, versatile resource not crystallized into a specific, specialized form with limited potential uses, and our situation at that edge of time which we call the present, is complex and many-stranded, and perhaps subtle and difficult to pin down in a succinct formula. Yet it is obvious and unmistakable. It is the epistemic aspects of money which are central and essential to the theme of the *General Theory*, but Keynes's instinctive contact with this truth is sometimes lost or overlaid, and seldom made explicit. It is vividly present at one point of the *Treatise*, in the penetrating account of the determination of bond prices by the conflicting expectations of Bulls and Bears. It is a truth hinted at by Wicksell in *Geldzins und Güterpreise*,[4] and brilliantly clarified as the upshot of an intense intellectual struggle by Myrdal in *Monetary Equilibrium*[5] and its Swedish and German earlier versions. *Ex ante* and *ex post* by its inspired lucidity could have saved Keynes and his readers vast labour and frustrations.

2. New tools in the *Treatise on Money*

Let us treat certain words for a moment as though they were elements in an axiom system, each defined only by its relation to other elements. Let us say that a society's income is the money measure of its annual production, that its saving is the excess of its income over its annual expenditure on consumption, and that its investment is the excess of its production, measured in money, over its consumption measured in money. Then it will be a pure tautology, a theorem derivable from the axioms, to say that saving is identically equal to investment. Saving and investment, in this system of terms, are two names for the same thing, and the things they name, being one and the same thing, cannot differ from each other in size. Yet in that chapter which is the core and kernel of the *Treatise on Money*, chapter 10 containing the Fundamental Equations for the Value of Money, we find that saving and investment can differ in their respective measurements. How did Keynes contrive so to define them that they can be unequal? The answer leads us to a fascinating and tantalizing conclusion. When he had written book III of the *Treatise*, Keynes was poised and equipped to inaugurate, or at least to duplicate, an analysis in terms of the bifocal view of an interval of time, the recognition that the expected and the recorded content of a named and identified segment of the calendar are different in nature. Investment and saving in the *Treatise* can be unequal because income does not there mean the value of production realized by sale of the product, but the value of production anticipated by enterprisers when they are *deciding* how much to produce. Income, in the Fundamental Equations, is a conjecture which can be wrong. The degree of its wrongness is profit, positive or negative; windfall profit; unexpected profit. In the *Treatise on Money*, income is defined ex ante, but expenditure is defined ex post. In the first Fundamental Equation (see pages 18–20 below) there are two terms. The first is the expected cost of production; the second is the amount by which the realized sale-proceeds diverge from that expectation. Keynes in the Fundamental Equations has engaged in sequence analysis, the viewing of a given interval from its threshold through the eyes of the participant, the enterpriser, the expectation-former and decision-maker, and the viewing of that same interval again from its termination; the viewing of it through the eyes of the book-keeper; and finally the comparison of those views, the drawing of inference from that comparison and the basing of new decisions on it. Keynes at the moment of writing his fundamental equations was all set (and this was in the late nineteen twenties) to make sequence analysis explicit. He did not do so, but Myrdal did. These two writers were neck-and-neck on the track, but one of them mistook the goal. Keynes swerved aside to write the *General Theory*, with its strange and perverse resort to identical equalities as though they could serve as conditions to be fulfilled. The arguments of the *Theory* are elliptical, and in order to accept them we must spell them out and supply the missing steps. The language in which they need to be spelt out is the language of expectation and the comparison of expectation with the record.

In the first three sections of chapter 10 of the *Treatise on Money*, together with the definition of income from chapter 9, and a passage on profits also from that chapter, we find a concise, complete theory of the sources, and the anatomy, of the movements of the aggregative variables in whose terms an economic society can be described. This theory draws its meaning from the consideration of what people think and feel. The explanation that it offers is in terms of the predicament in which men find themselves in this life, of having to act without knowing what will be the sequel of their acts, of having to exploit and take measures against an irremediable, perpetually renewed insufficiency of knowledge. The explanation is in terms of decision, of liquidity, of bearishness and bullishness, of speculation whether looked upon as defensive or gain-seeking. The account of things which is found in these brief pages is spare and condensed to the ultimate degree, it contains but only just contains the bare minimal outfit of ideas to serve its purpose. All that the *Treatise* says and all that the *General Theory* says is present in embryo in this capsule of thought. These claims are bold and I shall try to spell them out.

Our first proposition is that in the *Treatise on Money*, *income* is ex ante. Keynes says:

> 'We propose to mean identically the same thing by the three expressions : (1) the community's money income ; (2) the earnings of the factors of production ; and (3) the cost of production ; and we reserve the term *profits* for the difference between the cost of production of the current output and its actual sale proceeds, so that profits are not part of the community's income. The entrepreneurs being themselves amongst the factors of production, their normal remuneration is included in income, and, therefore, in the cost of production. But we exclude the windfall profits or losses represented by the difference (positive or negative) between the earnings of the factors of production and the actual sale proceeds. I define the 'normal' remuneration of entrepreneurs at any time as that rate of remuneration which, if they were open to make new bargains with the factors of production at the currently prevailing rates of earnings, would leave them under no motive either to increase or to decrease their scale of operations.' (pp. 111, 112)

We see that entrepreneurs' normal remuneration is defined by treating it as an *incentive*. It is therefore something whose nature consists in its being looked forward to. It may or may not, in the event, ex post, prove to be equal to the actual outturn. 'Normal remuneration' is something seen *ex ante*.

Next we learn that profit, existing only in the backward look at an interval which has elapsed, can influence decision concerning an interval which is to come. And we learn that the individual firm will thus decide the output and the employment it shall undertake : 'Thus when the actual rate of entrepreneurs' remuneration exceeds (or falls short of) the normal as thus defined, so that profits are positive (or negative) entrepreneurs will seek to expand (or curtail) their scale of operation at the existing costs of production'. (p. 112)

Thus far we are carried by the definitions of chapter 9. They have staged the play in an expectational and a sequence-analysis setting. Keynes of course did not use the term sequence analysis. I do not doubt that he would have rejected it. He preferred and preserved the freedom and fluidity of thought that verbal language by its manifold connections and suggestions of meaning can allow, and an aspect of this policy was the marked avoidance of a formal frame of calendar-ideas. He relied upon such words as *current*, *normal*, *actual*, which convey time-ideas by suggestion rather than definition, and which allow the reader to follow a swift march of thought without tripping over niceties, but which still have, in the end, to be precisely squared and fitted to each other, if we are to feel fully at ease with them. I shall try to show that, in fact, Keynes's construction of his Fundamental Equations is perfectly apt to be expressed in a formal sequence analysis. Indeed, it is a wonderfully felicitous abridgment and simplification of a quite difficult line of reasoning, fitting it admirably for comprehension by the busy administrator.

The quantities composing Keynes's First Fundamental Equation are as follows:

E   the total money income or earnings of the community in a unit of time.

I′ the part of E which [is associated with] the production of investment goods. Then E − I′ is the cost of production of consumption goods.

S   savings, the sum of the differences between the money incomes of individuals and their expenditure on consumption.

Then E − S measures the expenditure of income on consumption goods.

O the total output of goods expressed in units of cost of production.

R the output of consumption goods.

C the output of investment goods.

Then O = R + C.

P the price level of consumption goods.

In writing out Keynes's definitions, I have omitted the word 'current', and, except in one place, 'in a unit of time'. All the quantities composing the equation, except P, are flows, that is, quantities of dimension xt^{-1}, where x may be, for example, units of value or of some physical measure, and t is units of time-lapse. The First Fundamental Equation consists, on its right-hand side, purely of quantities in which the idea 'per unit of time' is implicit or is expressed. But the words *income* and *output* contain this meaning in themselves, and do not need 'per unit of time'. 'Savings per unit of time' and 'production per unit of time' would be correct, but Keynes sometimes uses instead the word 'current'. This seems to me an evasion. To measure income, output, expenditure, we must state the length of the time-interval involved. But in some contexts we must also state, in *respect of each symbol*, whether this interval has elapsed or is about to be traversed. 'Current' seems designed to leave unanswered the question whether the quantities are ex ante or ex post. It would be fairer to say, however, that this question is not deliberately evaded by Keynes and many other writers, but is entirely non-existent in their thought. The motion of a planet round its orbit can be, and is, described without reference to a particular position in that orbit or to the question of past and future. It is highly dangerous to carry over into human affairs, where the gaining of knowledge (including, and most especially, knowledge which is *new* not merely for the individual, and may subvert existing 'knowledge') belongs to the essence and the heart of the matter, and past and future are different in nature, the technique of differential equations where time is purely a dimension.

The First Fundamental Equation reads:

$$P = \frac{E}{O} + \frac{I' - S}{R} \quad \dots\dots\dots\dots (i)$$

Let us express its meaning in sequence analysis language. On the right-hand side we have two terms. The first is total income divided by total output. Income we remember is *expected* income. It is not something guaranteed to be realised and right. It consists of wages, salaries and rents promised by the entrepreneurs to their employees and other suppliers of means of production, and of their own remuneration, their 'normal' remuneration, namely that remuneration the *hope or assumption* of which has induced them to set their intended production at the level they have chosen. The first term, E/O, is an *expectation which can be wrong*. The second term is written-in, as it were, at a different date from that at which the first term is set down. The first term is written down (as a statement of what is being assumed by the entrepreneurs, what they are adopting as the basis of the decisions which, willy nilly, they must make) at the threshold of the time-interval. The second term cannot be written in until the interval has been traversed and what has occurred in it is on the record. The second term is the difference between what was expected at the threshold and what has happened in fact. The equation as a whole shows the price level of consumption-goods as dependent on their own quantity per time-unit and on the quantity of money expended on them in this same time-unit, the same not only in length but in identity as part of the calendar. That total expenditure on consumption-goods can be deemed to consist of two parts. One part is the spending on consumption-goods of the expected earnings from the process of producing consumption-goods. The other part is the spending on consumption-goods of part of the expected earnings from the process of production of investment-goods. If some of the earnings from the production of investment-goods are spent on consumption-goods, how is that part of the investment-goods which corresponds to this diverted expenditure to be bought? It is bought out of entrepreneurs' reserves of wealth, which they either have at hand in the form of money or can turn into money by the sale of existing assets; or it is bought out of money which is created at the entrepreneurs' instance by the banks. When, to the money earned in producing consumables, there is added a stream of money fed in from a standing reservoir, the total stream of consumption-expenditure will be greater than the expected stream which induced the flow of consumption-goods put on to the market in the just-elapsed interval. The price realised ex post will be greater than the cost of production counted on ex ante. A profit will have emerged, an *unexpected, windfall* profit.

The formula we have reproduced, which Keynes labels as equation (i), divides the influences which have determined the price-level of consumption goods into the expected and the unexpected part. The unexpected part can either increase the price level above what would have satisfied the entrepreneurs that their chosen output was right, or can sink it below that level. This division of the two influences into expected and unexpected also divides the total flow of money which is seen, at the end of the interval, to have in fact come forward to buy consumption goods, into the part which can be deemed to come from the income earned in producing consumption goods, and the part (positive or negative) which can be deemed to have come from the income earned in producing investment goods. For if, reversing Keynes's presentation, we multiply each side of equation (i) by R, the quantity of consumption goods which has been produced and sold to consumers, we have

$$P.R = \frac{E}{O}R + I' - S$$

Here $P.R$ is the price per unit of consumption goods times the number of units sold, that is to say, $P.R$ is the total expenditure which has been made in the just-elapsed interval on consumption-goods. E/O is the production cost per unit of goods of both sorts (the quantities of both sorts being measured in cost-of-production units), and R being the quantity which has been produced of consumption-goods, $(E/O).R$ is the total production cost of consumption-goods, the amount which, if realized by sale, would have just provided for the payment of wages, salaries, et cetera, and the precisely-sufficient remuneration of entrepreneurs in view of the output they chose. I′ is the corresponding production cost of investment-goods. However, only such part of this can be deemed to have been spent on consumption-goods as is left when we subtract S, saving. For we have made no allowance, in the term $(E/O).R$, for any saving out of income earned in producing consumables. Thus in the form

$$P.R = \frac{E}{O}.R + I' - S,$$

the First Fundamental Equation exhibits the total ex post expenditure on consumption goods as composed of earnings in the production of consumption-goods plus a possible addition, or a possible deduction, coming from the excess of investment earnings over total savings.

Keynes has great insights still to extract from the First Fundamental Equation, and we may be audacious enough to put our own gloss on those insights, and to go further still, and show the First Fundamental Equation as part of a still larger whole which can be discerned lying behind and around it, the full picture of sequence-analysis. But before we proceed to those developments, we must notice some features and peculiarities, and answer some questions, about what we have got already.

First, there is an aspect of the First Fundamental Equation which belongs precisely to the character we are suggesting for it of sequence analysis. Sequence analysis essentially consists in supposing all that occurs in a particular, 'proper-named' time-interval, to be the consequence of the inter-action of decisions taken, or left in force, at the threshold of that interval. Just so, Keynes in his equation is implicitly supposing that the entrepreneurs decide, in advance of the interval, how much to produce of consumption goods, and that they stick to the

decision as the interval elapses. Having labelled part of their
intended production as consumption-goods, they insist on selling that quantity, or an equal quantity, to consumers during
the interval. They do not allow any piling-up of unsold goods
which had been intended for consumption; they do not allow
any goods to be transferred, within the interval, from the
consumption-category to the investment category. The initi-
ally-planned output of consumption goods is not only actually
produced in the interval but is thrust upon consumers for
whatever price it will fetch.

A question sometimes raised about the Fundamental Equations concerns Keynes's method of measuring output. His
words are : 'Let us choose our units of quantities of goods in
such a way that a unit of each has the same cost of production
at the base date'. It is obvious that this method is adopted
faute de mieux. The problem of *scalarizing* a diverse collection
comprising tens of thousands of physically diverse items, when
such measures as mass or volumes are irrelevant, cannot be
solved precisely. The fact that economics is prepared to solve it
by something far short of a logically rigorous procedure is, perhaps, the most characteristic feature of our discipline. Economics might with some justice call itself the science of imprecision. It is faced with problems which can only be in some
degree trampled on, not solved. But if it is to exist at all, if it is
to offer solutions and policy recommendations which are sufficiently simple to be trusted by practical men, this trampling
must be done. It *is* done on every hand. The index-number
problem is accepted as a challenge to ingenuity, the man who
devises a particularly plausible argument and formula is as
proud of it as a Cordon Bleu cook with a new recipe. Keynes's
procedure is incisive and it is perfectly adapted to his purpose.
For the Fundamental Equation sets out to explain what
happens in a single, historically identifiable, proper-named
interval. The events of that interval are the upshot of decisions
all taken (we are free to suppose) at one and the same threshold moment. The fact that they are then taken, and contracts with suppliers of productive services then agreed, means

that costs of production can then be determined.

They can be determined, but what determines them? Must it not be the conditions of supply and demand which prevailed in the factor markets in the preceding time interval, and the legacy of wage-rates and other factor rewards which that interval bequeathed to this one? If the Fundamental Equations are to serve as a sequence analysis, they must be placed in a historical setting, where the out-turn of one interval is appealed to as the source of the expectations and prices that colour people's thoughts in taking their decisions for the next. Keynes does not articulate the historical process explicitly in these terms, but he constantly invokes the notion that the entrepreneurs' endeavours to expand production, in order to exploit the seeming possibilities of still greater gain suggested by the occurrence of a windfall profit in a just-elapsed interval, will drive up the rates of pay which they offer to suppliers of means of production. In pages 134 to 141, both inclusive, there are five passages of which the following is typical:

'Under a socialist system the money rate of efficiency earnings of the factors of production might be suddenly altered by *fiat*. It might change under a system of competitive individualism by a coup de main on the part of trade unions. [But] the most usual and important occasion of change will be the action of entrepreneurs, under the influence of the actual enjoyment of positive or negative profits, in increasing or diminishing the volume of employment which they offer at the existing rates of remuneration of the factors of production, and so bringing about a raising or lowering of these rates. It is by altering the rate of profits in particular directions that entrepreneurs can be induced to produce this rather than that, and it is by altering the rate of profits in general that they can be induced to modify the average of their offers of remuneration to the factors of production.'

The price-level of consumption-goods, which is thrown up by the decisions and interactions of a named historical interval, in a manner exhibited by the First Fundamental Equation, evidently depends on both the terms of that equation, both the expected unit cost of production, E/O, and the unexpected departure of the price from that unit cost, namely $(I' - S)/R$. Keynes of course makes this explicit. He first defines W as the rate of earnings per unit of human effort and W_1 as the rate of earnings per unit of output, namely 'the rate of efficiency earnings', and also e as the coefficient of efficiency such that $W = e \cdot W_1$. Equation (i) can then be re-written

$$P = W_1 + \frac{I' - S}{R}$$

$$= \frac{1}{e}W + \frac{I' - S}{R}$$

Here the first term is the price W of a unit of human effort multiplied by the number $1/e$ of units of human effort required per unit of output. Keynes proceeds:

'The price level of consumption goods (i.e. the inverse of the purchasing power of money) is made up, therefore, of two terms, the first of which represents the level of efficiency earnings, i.e. the cost of production, and the second of which is positive, zero or negative, according as the cost of new investment exceeds, equals or falls short of the volume of current savings. It follows that the stability of the purchasing power of money involves the two conditions — that efficiency earnings should be constant and that the cost of new investment should be equal to the volume of current savings.'

I claimed above that these pages of the *Treatise* from chapters 9 and 10 contain a complete macro-dynamic theory, a formal frame able to find a place for all questions about the movements of the great aggregative variables. The burning question of to-day is the source and nature of inflation. It is said to have two origins, cost-push and demand-pull. Such conceptual separation does not mean, of course, that they work in mutual isolation. Ultimately all economic elements are parts of the sensitive spider's-web of signalling-channels and currents of influence. But they may be said to bear upon different sides of the market, the supply-side and the demand-side. In this sense we can locate them both in the First Fundamental Equation. Cost-push, and every influence which bears upon and engenders it, is manifested in the first term. Demand-pull and everything which proximately governs it is manifested in the second. Keynes is at first mainly concerned with the latter. Yet if the Fundamental Equations are to become a complete statement of sequence analysis, they must be supplemented with some treatment of the influence of the *price-level* engendered by one interval on the *efficiency-earnings* prevailing in the next. It is here that we see the need, that I have been insisting on, to regard the intervals as belonging to a real historical sequence and not merely as anonymous portions of an abstract and eventless time.

We come then to the heart of the matter, the source and engenderment of demand-pull. And here we have in embryo the Multiplier theorem, the idea that when intended investment outgrows the assumptions of the providers of consumption-goods, those providers will soon find themselves encouraged to expand production, if they can. Keynes did not in the *Treatise* follow up this idea in detail, for the good reason that the *Treatise* had posed itself the question of the price-level and not that of the size of *output as a whole*. But the passage at the bottom of page 112, which I quoted, gives us all we need. If a positive windfall will induce entrepreneurs to 'seek to expand their scale of operations' (and a negative one will do the reverse) it is clear that windfall profits can raise or lower output as a whole when factors of production are available. The *Treatise* contains no suggestion of a Multiplier mechanism such as Lord Kahn provided in the following year. But a place for that structure was awaiting it. The Multiplier is the process of engenderment of extra output of consumers' goods as a consequence of the spending of incomes earned in the production of an extra flow of investment-goods; goods, that is, which cannot absorb any expenditure by consumers as such. The

multiplier mechanism is driven by a new extra flow of investment. We come, then, to the inducement to invest.

If a single concept were sought, which we should claim as
the most original and the most influential to be found in the
Treatise on Money or the *General Theory of Employment,
Interest and Money*, my own choice unquestionably would be
liquidity preference. This is the soul of Keynes's theory. Its
ascendancy depends upon a further idea, a much less technical,
more universally relevant truth, a truth about what Edward
FitzGerald called the Scheme of Things Entire, meaning the
human predicament and the bonds of existence. That truth
is our essential, incurable and merciful un-knowledge of what
may be the sequel of our choices of action. We cannot be eye-
witnesses of the future. The future if we take the word literally is something which *is not yet*. To speak of witnessing it
would be a contradiction in terms. Our conception of history-
to-come is necessarily figment, however subtly we combine
the evidence provided by the past, and despite the reliance we
can and must place on the regularities of the physical world.
Those regularities are like rigid, precisely-shaped building
blocks, with which, despite their definite and stable individual
form, buildings of infinite variety can be built.

Liquidity is that property of some assets, and most notably,
of money, which fits them to serve as a refuge for the wealth
of individual persons or firms when the uncertainty of things
has suddenly unmasked itself with special insistence. At
moments when 'the news' is especially confusing, the scene
of political, technological or social affairs particularly obscure
and unresolvable, it seems possible for an individual to avoid
many hazards by holding money instead of technically specific
property, particular kinds of tools, buildings or facilities. In
order to do so, those who own such equipment, directly or as
shareholders, must sell it. When a general movement to sell
occurs, the prices of such assets in terms of money, and also in
comparison with the money-cost of producing them, will go
down. It will cease to be worthwhile to produce such goods,
because their market value is now less than the market value

of the means of making them. The production of such goods, the production of investment-goods, will decline. A retreat from investment is of course a retreat from employment.

If we sought to condense Keynes's whole thesis concerning employment into a single sentence, we might say that he ascribes the possibility of involuntary general unemployment to the existence of a liquid asset in a world of uncertainty. Liquidity of course would have no meaning in any other world. Yet the two elements are conceptually distinct. Their separateness appears in the relative attention they get in the *Treatise* and in the *General Theory*. In the *Treatise*, which is *about* money, it is natural that the emphasis should be upon liquidity itself, its existence and effect. In the *Treatise* there is begun the discussion of the securities market as a speculative market with 'two views', such that the banking system, by showing greater or less readiness to meet the desire of the Bears for savings deposits, can influence the price of securities and the inducement to invest. But in the *Treatise* we find little about the uncertainty which gives liquidity its meaning. It is in the *General Theory*, and above all in the QJE,[2] that we find the appeal to uncertainty, to un-knowledge of the outcomes of available courses of action, as the origin of the difficulty of maintaining the flow of investment at a level which can engender full employment in face of a given and considerable propensity to save.

Liquidity preference first appears in the *Treatise*:

'When a man is deciding what proportion of his money income to save, he is choosing between present consumption and the ownership of wealth. In so far as he decides in favour of consumption, he must necessarily purchase goods —for he cannot consume money. But in so far as he decides in favour of saving, there still remains a further decision for him to make. For he can own wealth by holding it either in the form of money or in other forms of loan or real capital. There is a further significant difference between the two types of decision. The decision as to the volume of saving,

and also the decision as to the volume of new investment,
relate wholly to current activities. But the decision as to
holding bank deposits or securities relates, not only to the
current increment to the wealth of individuals, but also to
the whole block of their existing capital. Indeed, since the
current increment is but a trifling proportion of the block of
existing wealth, it is but a minor element in the matter.
Now when an individual is more disposed than before to
hold his wealth in the form of savings deposits and less disposed to hold it in other forms, this does not mean that he
is determined to hold it in the form of savings deposits *at all
costs*. It means that he favours savings deposits (for whatever reason) more than before at the existing price level of
other securities. But his distaste for other securities is not
absolute and depends on his expectations of the future
return to be obtained from savings deposits and from other
securities respectively, which is obviously affected by the
price of the latter. If, therefore, the price level of other
securities falls sufficiently, he can be tempted back into
them. Thus the change in the relative attractions of savings
deposits and securities has to be met either by a fall in the
prices of securities or by an increase in the supply of savings
deposits. A fall in the price level of securities is therefore an
indication that the 'bearishness' of the public has been in-
sufficiently offset by the creation of savings deposits by the
banking system.' (pp. 127–8)

The words *liquidity* and *liquidity-preference* name a complex skein of subtle and elusive ideas. Our brief quoted passage
touches on a surprising proportion of them, and implicitly
suggests the very questions which Keynes's later discussions,
in the *Treatise* and in the *General Theory*, have sought to
answer. In this passage he refutes in advance those with whom
he spent much space in argument in the *Economic Journal* of
1937,[3] the loanable-funds theorists who declared that the
interest-rate was determined at the level where it brought to
equality merely the demand and the supply of new loans. In

that volume of the *Journal* Ohlin says:

> 'What governs the demand and supply of credit? Two ways
> of reasoning are possible. One is *net* and deals only with *new*
> credit, and the other is *gross* and includes the outstanding
> *old* credits. The willingness of certain individuals during a
> given period to increase their holdings of various claims and
> other kinds of assets minus the willingness of others to re-
> duce their corresponding holdings gives the supply curves
> for the different kinds of new credit during the period.
> Naturally, the quantities each individual is willing to supply
> depend on the interest-rates. The total supply of *new* claims
> minus the reduction in the oustanding volume of old ones
> gives the demand—also a function of the rates of interest
> —for the different kinds of credit during the period. A
> similar kind of reasoning can of course be applied gross, i.e.
> including the old claims which were outstanding when the
> period began. It is quite obvious (Ohlin proceeds) that this
> reasoning in gross terms leads to the same result as the net
> analysis above.'

What is obvious, we may say, is that Ohlin and Keynes were
talking at cross-purposes, and it is unprofitable to try to disentangle their misconceptions of each other's meaning. But it
is also plain that the view which Ohlin expresses in this
passage was totally at odds with the meaning, origin and implications of liquidity preference. Ohlin here thinks of the
bond market as behaving like a market for flows of perishable
commodities. But bonds are not perishable in the sense that
tomatoes are. To dismiss, as Ohlin does, the existence of old
bonds as negligible and irrelevant is to miss the whole point,
the heart and essence of the matter, the fact, namely, that the
bond market is a *speculative* market. Bonds are not valued by
the pressures of unstorable supplies and unsurvivable hunger
They are not valued as *flows*. Ohlin's *period* is beside the
point. The securities newly created this week or even this year
are overshadowed by the mountainous bulk of existing assets
All those 'old' assets can always and at any time be thrown on

the market. Most essential of all is the contrast in the manner of response of markets for flows and markets for stocks. Markets for flows respond *essentially* in the volume, as well as in the price, of transactions. This response takes time. But markets for stocks can respond instantly, literally with the speed of thought, for speculative prices depend on thoughts, namely, on expectations of future possible prices. Speculators who have decided to sell may find that their own revaluations have already been paralleled in the minds of potential buyers, and sale is not worth while.

Keynes's passage contains the notion of the price of securities having to respond to two influences : firstly, the individual's expectations of the future return to be obtained from savings deposits and from other securities respectively, these expectations being thought of as themselves depending on circumstances ; and secondly, the chief of those circumstances, namely, the abundance or otherwise of savings deposits, the readiness or reluctance of the banking system to create them. Are we, then, to think of the price of securities as a function of the size of the stock of money, or rather of that part of it which is not occupied in mediating transactions? Here Keynes seems divided in mind. There is here, we may think, a contest in his mind between the expediency of method and the principle of meaning. Keynes, deeply Marshallian, found it congenial and almost unavoidable to think in terms of two variables at a time, each a function of the other, each able, according to the purposes of the moment, to be regarded as 'dependent on' the other. Yet he was perfectly aware, as he says in the *Treatise*, that this two-by-two functionality was a mere intellectual device:

'It follows that the actual price level of investments is the resultant of the sentiment of the public and the behaviour of the banking system. This does not mean that there is any definite numerical relationship between the price level of investments and the additional quantity of savings deposits created. The amount by which the creation of a given quantity of deposits will raise the price of other securities above what their price would otherwise have been depends on the shape of the public's demand curve for savings deposits at different price levels of other securities.' (p. 128)

There is an internal contradiction in this passage as it stands. If the public's attitude or sentiment can be expressed by a unique curve of given and stable form, then we could read off from this curve, if we had it before our eyes, the 'amount by which the creation of a given quantity of deposits will raise the price of other securities'. Yet stability and constancy of form is the very last thing we can attribute to such a curve. For that curve will be deformed and displaced in any manner and degree by 'the news', the straws in the wind that are all that reality gives us as a stand-in for that mythical full information assumed by timeless value-theory. Such a liquidity-curve is a mere thread floating in the wind, responding in its changes of shape to every breath of fresh expectation. The dilemma that Keynes's reference to this curve glosses over is a dilemma which runs through the whole of the *General Theory*. It appears dramatically in his account of the inducement to invest, which is the concern of the next chapter.

3. The theory of investment. Form without Content?

What determines the extent by which a society improves or enlarges its productive equipment in a year? We have here sought to construct the most question-begging question that can be achieved in small compass on what the economist calls *investment*. In this formula there are at least three words which call for query, objection or examination. Several questions can be asked about each of them, not by way of hair-splitting quibbles but because these words, if we may be allowed a paradox, make a parade of their hidden assumptions or pre-conceptions. What does 'determine' mean? What are the conditions which must be fulfilled before we can claim that some quantity is 'determined'? What is achieved by showing how something is determined? 'Extent' is a word which plainly postulates scalar, that is, one-dimensional, quantity or measurement. Is productive equipment, in its ineffable diversity of form, ingredients, purposes, a suitable object of scalar measurement? The expression 'in a year' is of course meant to specify the dimension of the quantity we are concerned with, to indicate that if x is a symbol for quantity of equipment and t a symbol for time-lapse, investment will be of dimension xt^{-1}. But when we say 'a year' are we thinking of a stationary state where it does not matter which particular year is chosen, or where indeed there are no particular years since all are alike? Or are we thinking of a proper-named historical year, say 1972, located in the calendar? Or are we thinking of 'the year about to be entered upon'? It makes a difference to our conception of what is involved in the idea of *determination.*

To determine a quantity is to place bounds upon it, to

ascertain that it lies between such-and-such marks on a scale. We need not compare it with the scale directly. We may have some verbal or algebraic expression which, given that some quantities are known, enables us to calculate the quantity in question. This second meaning of 'determine' suggests that the quantity to be ascertained is looked on as a member of some class of measurements, all of whose members refer to the same kind of measurable thing or the same set of circumstances of measurement: that the quantity to be ascertained is a *value of a variable*. Then it follows that some of the data for calculating our quantity will also be variable quantities, classes of measurements rather than single specimens, and the expression which gives instructions for the calculation will be a *function*. The character and ingredients of this function may easily be more interesting to the economist than any numerical result he can obtain by using it. For the character and ingredients of this function (its parameters and its list of arguments or 'independent' variables, respectively) reflect and express a conception of how the society in question, in its economic aspects, operates and hangs together, a conception of its structure. And to know this structure, to have insight into what depends on what, what is influenced or governed by what, is one of the chief concerns of the theoretician. The insidious dangers are deeper than his merely being satisfied with empty boxes. He may say to himself 'If some of these variable quantities, on which the size of the flow of investment can be taken to depend, can be assumed to move only a little during some period, then by manipulating some one or more of the other variables we may be able to influence or control the investment-flow'. If some of the argument-variables ('independent variables') can be assumed to stay put for some 'short period', then it may not matter whether or not they can be measured. Policy recommendations in terms of some supposedly manipulable variables will seem to have some validity. The question whether and why other variables can be neglected is liable itself to be neglected.

One further temptation besets the economist. He is very

fond of doing sums. If the supposed formula for determining the annual aggregate expenditure on improving or enlarging the society's equipment offers interesting sums, there will be a temptation to take the answers to these sums as fact. In book IV of the *General Theory*, called The Inducement to Invest, we see an arresting contrast. It is the contrast between the incisive formula offered in that book IV as an account of the determination of investment, on one hand; and on the other, the theme which Keynes clothes in uncompromising and mind-shaking words, not once but repeatedly: the theme of the evanescence, the elusiveness and capacity for instantaneous transformation, which inheres in any structure of expectations, any momentary vista of possible sequels to possible present action; the expectations which are the sole means of filling the empty boxes of the formula, and which are its effective content as distinct from its formal specification. The formula itself is easy to state. Having defined the marginal efficiency of capital, (a definition which we will examine below) Keynes says:

'Now it is obvious that the actual rate of current investment will be pushed to the point where there is no longer any class of capital asset [no kind of equipment] of which the marginal efficiency exceeds the current rate of interest. In other words, the rate of investment will be pushed to the point on the investment demand-schedule where the marginal efficiency of capital in general is equal to the market rate of interest.' (p. 136)

What could seem more incisive? If only we know the investment demand-schedule and the rate of interest, everything will be easy. So what does Keynes tell us about the investment demand-schedule, the function relating the marginal efficiency of capital to the size of the investment-flow? What he tells us reveals a sea of doubts, difficulties and begging of questions, not disguised by him (far from it) but thrown into a somewhat misleading perspective by another obvious fact: that about the ultimate source and nature of ideas which may influence the marginal efficiency of capital, there is almost nothing *general* to be said except that expectation is the play of the mind over what is essentially a void; the play of thought constrained only by fragmentary fact interpreted by more or less obsolete experience. About the interpretive process, or rather the process of making bricks with little straw, there is for the economist almost nothing to be said (Keynes's renunciation of the problem occupies only a footnote of 95 words, footnote 3 on page 24 of the *General Theory*) and when there is nothing to be said about a subject, you cannot make that subject seem important (no matter how truly and essentially important, as in this case, it really is) by spending pages and chapters on it. On the other hand, about the interest-rate there is any amount to be said, and it occupies three chapters containing a total of 45 pages, not including the famous chapter 17. Thus a superficial reading of the *General Theory* may give the impression that the interest-rate is what matters in the governance of investment. Keynes sometimes goes far to rebut this view (*General Theory*, page 145 line 25). But he cannot avoid the effect of bulk in producing an impression of dominant importance.

> 'When a man buys an investment or capital asset, [Keynes says in the first sentence of book IV] he purchases the right to the series of prospective returns, which he expects to obtain from selling its output, after deducting the running expenses of obtaining that output, during the life of the asset. This series of annuities $Q_1, Q_2, \ldots, Q_n$ it is convenient to call the *prospective yield* of the investment.'

Yield is perhaps not the happiest choice of name for the series of Q's, since that term through customary usage suggests a ratio between two things, whereas the Q's are simple amounts of value. But so long as we are clear that the Q's are differences obtained, one for each future year, by subtracting supposed operating costs of the equipment from supposed sale-proceeds of the goods it produces, the name is a matter of taste. There are more vital matters. If the reader or hearer feels impatient at the spending of time on textual criticism, let me urge that the meaning, the ideas themselves of our theories can be given transmissible form, can be recorded and conveyed only by words or word-equivalent symbols. We depend on the words and must study them. In Keynes's sentence just quoted there are the words 'prospective' and 'expected', and there are the symbols Q_1, Q_2, ..., Q_n, whose respective numerical values can in general differ from each other, but which, each taken by itself, calls to the reader's mind the idea of a single number. Each Q, so far as our quoted sentence goes, stands for a *single-valued expectation*. How, then, by what consultation of evidence and what interpretive process applied to that evidence, by what systematic or haphazard or by what active or passive gathering of suggestions, by what mode of thought, are those single-valued expectations arrived at?

Keynes's dealings with uncertainty, with the essential plurality of answers which a man (if he is reasonable and cautious) is obliged to entertain concerning any question where the evidence is not unique in meaning, complete and conclusive, are bound to engage our curious attention. From the author of *A Treatise on Probability*, [7] the earliest of all his books, we might expect a close and ingenious study of how, out of an insufficiency of knowledge, rational, logically defensible guidance can be obtained. In the *General Theory* there is nothing of the sort. And in that 'third edition', that ultimate distillation of the *Treatise* and the *Theory*, which Keynes wrote for the *QJE* [6] in answer to his critics, there is something wholly different. There he tells how men deliberately and consciously, but with a powerful faculty of make-believe blind themselves to the fact of the unknown and unknowable future which lies only a little way out (in proportion to the human span) from our 'present moment', how they make life practicable and endurable by a convention:

'How do we manage in such circumstances to behave in a manner which saves our faces as rational economic men? We have devised for the purpose a variety of techniques, of

which much the most important are the three following:
(1) We assume that the present is a much more serviceable guide to the future than a candid examination of past experience would show it to have been hitherto. In other words we largely ignore the prospect of future changes about the actual character of which we know nothing.
(2) We assume that the existing state of opinion as expressed in prices and the character of existing output is based on a correct summing up of future prospects, so that we can accept it as such until something new and relevant comes into the picture.
(3) Knowing that our individual judgement is worthless, we endeavour to fall back on the judgement of the rest of the world, which is perhaps better informed. That is, we endeavour to conform with the behaviour of the majority or the average. The psychology of a society of individuals each of whom is endeavouring to copy the others leads to what we may strictly term a conventional judgement.

'Now, [Keynes proceeds] a practical theory of the future based on these three principles has certain marked characteristics. In particular, being based on so flimsy a foundation, it is subject to sudden and violent changes. The practice of calmness and immobility, of certainty and security, suddenly breaks down. New fears and hopes will, without warning, take charge of human conduct. The forces of disillusion may suddenly impose a new conventional basis of valuation. All these pretty, polite techniques, made for a well-panelled board-room and a nicely-regulated market, are liable to collapse. At all times the vague panic fears and equally vague and unreasoned hopes are not really lulled and lie but a little way below the surface.'

It has long appeared to me that Keynes's expositors, commentators and critics either contrive, for the sake of their peace of mind, to leave this passage unread, or else they turn aside as men who have looked over the edge into the abyss and must endeavour to blot this dreadful vision from their mind. For this passage pronounces the dissolution of the view of business conduct as rational, as the application to men's affairs of *fully-informed reason*. Yet it is the assumption that men act by fully-informed reason that underlies the whole of value-theory; that underlies what, until forty years ago, was virtually the whole of economic theory. What is General Equilibrium, if not the outcome of a carefully-organized pre-reconciliation of rational choices? When Keynes was alive, economists had opportunities of hearing what he said, but they did not believe he really meant it. 'Equilibrium is blither' he once orally remarked. Could value-theorists be expected to understand? Keynes was not, I believe, disparaging the force and beauty, the logic, ingenuity and encompassing power to unify and simplify the economic scene, which General Equilibrium possesses. He was saying, in effect, that the world thus illuminated is an artificial, abstract and remote conception, the mere profile of a shadow of reality, entirely misleading if we take it to be the whole truth.

The unleashed invective of the QJE [6] article is only faintly suggested by the more technical and reflective tone of the opening passages of chapter 12 of the book itself. [2] But these passages are important:

'It would be foolish, in forming our expectations, to attach great weight to matters which are very uncertain. It is reasonable, therefore, to be guided to a considerable degree by the facts about which we feel somewhat confident, even though they may be less decisively relevant to the issue than other facts about which our knowledge is vague and scanty. For this reason the facts of the existing situation enter, in a sense disproportionately, into the formation of our long-term expectations. The state of long-term expectation, upon which our decisions are based, does not solely depend, therefore, on the most probable forecast we can make. It also depends on the confidence with which we make the forecast—on how highly we rate the likelihood of our best forecast turning out quite wrong. The state of confidence, as they term it, is a matter to which practical men always pay the closest and most serious attention. But [Keynes continues] economists have not analysed it carefully and have been content, as a rule, to discuss it in general terms. In particular it has not been made clear that its relevance to economic problems comes in through its important influence on the schedule of the marginal efficiency of capital. There are not two separate factors affecting the rate of investment, namely, the schedule of the marginal efficiency of capital and the state of confidence. The state of confidence is relevant because it is one of the major factors determining the former, which is the same thing as the investment demand schedule.

The outstanding fact is the extreme precariousness of the basis of knowledge on which our estimates of prospective yield [the series of Q's] have to be made. Our knowledge of the factors which will govern the yield of an investment some years hence is usually very slight and often negligible. If we speak frankly, we have to admit that our basis of knowledge for estimating the yield ten years hence of a railway, a copper mine, the goodwill of a patent medicine, or a building in the City of London amounts to little and sometimes to nothing; or even five years hence.'

These lines contain some enigmas which it is essential to examine. They concern Keynes's use of the terms *uncertainty* and *schedule*. It is indeed the association of these words that poses the main difficulty and makes us wish to gloss his account. He speaks at the outset of 'matters which are very uncertain', and in a footnote explains that 'By "very uncertain" I do not mean the same thing as "very improbable".' The footnote refers us to the *Treatise on Probability*, chapter 6, on "The weight of arguments". In his *Treatise on Probability* Keynes's central and consistent purpose is to answer the very general question : What is the nature of the link between a given body of evidence and some proposition to which this evidence is taken to be relevant; and accordingly : What circumstances govern the degree of support which the evidence properly* gives to the proposition. This approach, by way of a question about a single proposition considered in its own right, is the one I have favoured in proposing *potential surprise*. However, this approach is liable to obscure the fact that when probability is being appealed to in Keynes's words as 'the guide of life', we are viewing each of several propositions as one of the rival answers to some question about the sequel to this or that available policy or course of conduct. There then enters into the matter the number and diversity of these rivals, or in special contexts, the quantitative range over which they are dispersed. This consideration leads to the first of the enigmas. In the *General Theory*, page 148 line 8, does 'very uncertain' mean : resting on evidence which may, at its face value, give the proposition or hypothesis a high probability, but evidence which is in its own nature and scope remote from conclusiveness; or does it mean that the proposition or hypothesis, being quantitative, has a number of rivals very widely different from itself? Evidently these two meanings are far from independent. There must be some incompleteness and inconclusiveness about a body of evidence which allows many widely diverse answers to one and the same question to hold the field together. If the body of evidence becomes more stringent, more nearly complete (but I enter a strong caveat concerning this dangerous phrase) will it not inevitably give to some one or more of the rival answers a better standing, a stronger ostensible claim to be the truth, than before, in comparison with the other answers? If so, there is a close positive association, in this category of cases, between what Keynes in the *Treatise on Probability* calls 'weight of arguments' and the degree of belief, the degree of probability, assigned to the most probable answer. When the weight or adjudged reliability of the evidence increases, it may be that the effective range of dispersion of answers may contract.

---

* Keynes speaks *passim* of 'degrees of *rational* belief'. Since I cannot accept his interpretation of this phrase I have here evaded the issue by means of 'properly'.

Nonetheless, the two meanings we have sought to discern in the term *uncertain* are distinct, and it is relevant to our examination of Keynes's account of the investment demand-schedule to consider what he had in mind.

I think that what Keynes had in mind is an aspect of what elsewhere I have ventured to call his kaleidic account of the economic process of history. By the kaleidic theory I mean the view that the expectations, which together with the drive of needs or ambitions make up the 'springs of action', are at all times so insubstantially founded upon data and so mutably suggested by the stream of 'news', that is, of counter-expected or totally unthought-of events, that they can undergo complete transformation in an hour or even a moment, as the patterns in the kaleidoscope dissolve at a touch; the view that men are conscious of their essential and irremediable state of un-knowledge and that they usually suppress this awareness in the interest of avoiding a paralysis of action; but that from time to time they succumb to its abiding mockery and menace, and withdraw from the field.

This in essence is the meaning I find in the passage I have quoted from the *QJE* and in chapter 12 of the *General Theory*. Uncertainty in this connection means two things, each leaning upon the other : the fragmentary, vague and illusory basis, and the scope which this gives for abruptly and unaccountably changing interpretation and construing of the meaning. Data and construction are almost indistinguishable, readily and inevitably mistaken for each other. More than that. Since another man's beliefs and consequent intentions, however ill-judged, are for me data which I must reckon with in deciding my own course, there is in truth no dividing line between what we are given to construe and the way we, as individuals influencing each other, construe it. Uncertainty is the kaleidic factor. The less the strength and power of conviction which the evidence shows in favour of one particular answer or hypothesis to our question : What will be the sequel if I do this? the greater the ease, the wider the scope, for me to switch my attention to another hypothesis. There are two facets to uncertainty, but they are two facets of one thing. Neither in the *Treatise on Probability*, where we turn for the pure theory of the matter, nor in the *General Theory*, where we seek its application, do we find the mode of insight which I am suggesting spelled out. In the *Treatise on Probability*, chapter 6 begins with diffidence : 'The question to be raised in this chapter is somewhat novel; after much consideration I remain uncertain as to how much importance to attach to it'. Yet at least in his discernment of practical effect, when he wrote for the *QJE*, Keynes was incisive and uncompromising to the last degree.

Uncertainty then, we seem bound to conclude, is a unity, though with many faces. But there is one statement that can I think be unequivocally made about it. When there is uncertainty in an individual's thoughts, when his state of mind is that of uncertainty, then necessarily his situation is that he faces a question to which he entertains, either explicitly and consciously or at least in principle and with a *potential* explicitness waiting to come to the surface, a number of rival, that is, mutually exclusive, answers, answers such that the truth of one implies the falsity of the others. Now if we derive from the quoted passage above from the *General Theory*, that Keynes envisaged a series of Q's, representing the supposed trading revenue of some enterprise at some given size of the investment-flow into plant of that kind, as a series of *unique* numbers, one number for each Q_i; if, that is, we believe the series of Q's at any one time-rate of investment to be *single-valued expectations*; how can this interpretation be reconciled with his massive and downright insistence on the uncertainty of such expectations, and by implication their *plurality in rivalry?* This is the first of our enigmas.

Let us remind ourselves of the formal frame of ideas. The enterpriser-investor is concerned with some one industry, and with the question whether or not to order the construction of a system of equipment, of given design and scale, to serve this industry. Keynes supposes him to arrive at a series of Q's for such a plant. Each Q_i refers to a particular calendar year *i* in the series stretching ahead from the present, and each is a single number standing for the excess of trading revenue over operating expense in that year, and is a supposition, a conjecture. The enterpriser has also in mind a supposition concerning the cost of acquirement of the plant. Some rate of discount applied to the Q's will bring the total of their present values to equality with the cost of acquirement. Such a discount rate is of course expressed conventionally as a percentage per annum, or a proper fraction per time unit. This rate of discount is the efficiency of capital, according to the enterpriser's expectations, if invested at his 'present' in this plant. Since there is a question whether this plant should be built or not, it is evidently marginal in the enterpriser's investment policy. In formulating that policy, and in arriving at the series of Q's for its marginal item of investment, he should have had regard to the possible or presumed investment intentions of other enterprisers in his industry and in industry at large; indeed, in the world at large. How can he possibly 'have regard' in any well-founded manner and meaningful sense? But that, of course, is the second of our enigmas.

In requiring him to 'have regard' to the intentions of others we are asking the impossible. It is only within a system of general pre-reconciliation of intentions, a system of general equilibrium achieved in a discontinuous market or its equivalent, that well-founded account can be taken by one individual of that part of the total circumstances of his own action which will be constituted by the actions of others. Such pre-reconciliation is conceivable when all the actions are simple exchanges of goods. For investment intentions there is no such market, for the Stock Exchange, as Keynes spends the bulk of chapter 12 of the *General Theory* in explaining, is not such a market. To speak of *the* marginal efficiency of capital is to appeal to equilibrium ideas which are wholly at odds with the spirit of Keynes's theme and argument. Each enterpriser can without inconsistency or absurdity be deemed to arrive at a personal marginal efficiency of capital. But this will be achieved by applying the private interpretive frame of his own experience to a body of evidence which is fragmentary and insubstantial even in regard to the present, and has nothing factual to say of the future. The marginal efficiency of capital exists in a private world and can stand at as many levels as there are individuals. Thus we are confronted with the second enigma of Keynes's theory of investment. Its *formal frame* is that of equilibrium, of rational, pre-reconciled and fully informed action. Its *meaning* is, that 'full information', in the context of the real human predicament, is a phrase reverberating with the laughter of the gods, a mockery of truth, an outright and essential impossibility.

To say that the individual enterpriser-investor will be unable effectively to take account of the investment-intentions of other enterprisers in his industry, is to say that he does not know whereabouts he is on the investment demand-schedule. Intersecting that schedule from below, we may suppose, there will be the schedule of the interest-rate considered as a function of the time-rate of investment in this industry. If we interpret Keynes's conception as particular equilibrium analysis, the interest-rate, being then assumed independent of this single industry's operations, may be a horizontal straight line. But our question is, how does our individual investor know whether, if he contributes to the industry's stream of investment by deciding to build his plant, the point representing the margin of the industry's investment-stream will prove to lie above and to the left or below and to the right of the intersection-point? And before we can even frame our question thus, there is another which gives it an air of elusiveness and of illusion. We have been speaking of the investment demand-schedule as though it were in some sense established and universally agreed, like a market price. How can it in fact be other than the private creation of an individual mind? Our modes of thought, and Keynes has not elected to escape them or has not succeeded, encourage us to imagine the economic decision maker as faced with ready-made and visible curves on which he can place his finger. Instead, he must first draw the curves himself from the suggestions offered by fragmentary evidence.

Keynes is fully seized, is a repeatedly and arrestingly eloquent exponent, of the dependence of his whole theme on expectation. Chapter 11 of the *General Theory*, the chapter called The Marginal Efficiency of Capital, ends as follows:

'The schedule of the marginal efficiency of capital [the schedule which expresses the marginal efficiency as a function of the time-rate of investment in equipment of the relevant kind] is of fundamental importance because it is mainly through this factor (much more than through the rate of interest) that the expectation of the future influences the present. The mistake of regarding the marginal efficiency of capital primarily in terms of the current yield of capital equipment, which would be correct only in the static state where there is no changing future to influence the present, has had the result of breaking the theoretical link between to-day and to-morrow. Even the rate of interest is, virtually, a *current* phenomenon; and if we reduce the marginal efficiency of capital to the same status, we cut ourselves off from taking any direct account of the influence of the future in our analysis of the existing equilibrium. It is by reason of the existence of durable equipment that the economic future is linked to the present. It is, therefore, consonant with, and agreeable to, our broad principles of thought, that the expectation of the future should affect the present through the demand-price for durable equipment.'

Keynes here uses the very words 'the existing *equilibrium*'. Yet what he is discussing is the answers *originated* by each business man to questions which have no means or possibility of factual, eye-witness answer, questions which can elicit only figments and hopes. There is, so far as I can see, only one interpretation we can put on 'equilibrium' that will reconcile it to this context. It must be understood as the ephemeral adjustment that may from time to time come about when, by accident or the felicity of chance, affairs are given a breathing-space and something resembling the Marshallian 'normal' can come about. These pauses in the cascade of history I have ventured to call kaleidic. It may be fair to say that Keynes in all this field has matched the elusiveness, the unseizableness of the ideas and problems by a masterly resort to elliptical language. When mankind cannot penetrate and dissect something, it copes with that difficulty as the oyster does with the intrusive particle of grit, by encapsulating it in a gleaming envelope, of pearl or of grammatical forms.

The difficulty of reconciling, on one hand, the notion of a schedule or curve unique and definite, which associates each distinct hypothetical time-rate of investment by the industry in its characteristic equipment with some one numerical value of the marginal efficiency of capital, and on the other hand that of the plurality and mutual exclusiveness of answers, which inheres in the notion of uncertainty, is an instance of a basic dilemma of the theory of knowledge, a general dilemma facing any discipline where human conjectural thought and decision play a part. This is the most fundamental of the problems that Keynes's treatment of investment-theory poses. The second problem exhibits this first one in a more special light. The unnaturalness of employing an equilibrium method in an expectational economics might more readily have struck Keynes and other economists, if there had been available any other approach which accorded human faculties some scope and influence in human affairs, and was not, like many business cycle theories, purely mechanical. Even the Keynes of the *Treatise on Money*, with its glimpses of sequence analysis and its vidid revelation of interest-rates as springing from defensive speculation, seems in the *General Theory* to accept equilibrium, in the technical, instrumental Marshallian sense, as imposing itself ineluctably. Yet a Marshallian partial equilibrium postulates, not provides, sufficient knowledge.

Keynes takes it for granted that a business man will assign smaller marginal efficiencies to capital which he might invest in his industry, the larger the flow of such investment by the industry as a whole which he assumes. The marginal efficiency of capital, that is to say, will be a decreasing function of the size of the industry's supposed investment-flow. On page

136 of the *General Theory* he says:

> 'If there is increased investment in any given type of capital
> during any given period of time the marginal efficiency of
> that type of capital will diminish as the investment in it is
> increased, partly because the prospective yield will fall as
> the supply of that type of capital [i.e. of equipment] is in-
> creased, and partly because, as a rule, pressure on the facili-
> ties for producing that type of capital will cause its supply-
> price to increase.'

Here it is evident that Keynes is engaging in *partial equilibrium* analysis. He speaks of investment in a 'given' type of
capital, that is of course, of equipment. And it is surely only
when the increased investment is done by a single industry, a
small part of the productive system as a whole, that the prospective yield (the series of Q's) will be a decreasing function
of the time-rate of the investment. For what of the effect of a
general increase of the pace of investment in all industries,
with its Multiplier effect on the size of general output as a
whole, to which Keynes has devoted the whole of his book III,
in bodily shifting upwards the revenue prospects and expectations of yield of investment of all the industries taken together?
Investment induces consumption, but does not consumption
induce investment?

We are here brought face to face with a remarkable feature,
which has remained almost unremarked, of the *General
Theory* in all of its main text excluding chapter 22. Except in
that chapter, Keynes nowhere touches on the question of the
influence of changes of output as a whole on the pace of investment (in contrast with the many pages and intensive discussion he devotes to the influence of changes in the pace of investment on the size of general output). And except in that
chapter, he will have no systematic truck with time-lagged
reactions. It is small wonder that those economists in 1936 and
the immediately following years who seized with greatest
readiness and delight upon the Keynesian cornucopia of ideas
were united in their conviction that here was an incomparable

means of new insight into the business cycle. Harrod (1936),[8] Samuelson (1939),[9] Kaldor (1940),[10] and Hicks (1950),[11] even the present writer (1938),[12] all produced theories of the business cycle drawing upon the liberative inspirations of the *General Theory*. Why did Keynes himself neglect, or even repudiate, these possibilities, except in a chapter called Notes on the Trade Cycle, in Book VI which is itself a sort of epilogue to the main thesis? My suggestion is that he wished the *General Theory of Employment, Interest and Money* to be an outfit of tools, possessed indeed of its own unity and self-sufficiency, possessed of a dominant and central theme, but not constituting a rigid model of economic society. Keynes believed in the eclectic use of *general ideas*, such ideas as the essentially speculative character of the interest rate, the mutable and precarious basis of the inducement to invest, the consequences of the existence of a liquid, non-specific asset, in order to analyse and prescribe for each and any situation as an individual problem in its own right, not as a mere illustration of some pre-ordained mode of history. Was he not justified in this view? To have made the *General Theory* just another theory of the trade cycle, another machine only capable of performing its routines, would have made it appear outdated from the outbreak of war and afterwards. Keynes wished to discover general truths, not to superpose upon them arbitrary and artificial constructions.

4. Interest rates in the *Treatise* and the *Theory*

Economics was for long divided into two provinces which seemed independent of each other. There was *value* and there was *money*. Value was about things useful and desirable by reason, as it seemed, of physical properties, things which nourish people or keep them warm or carry them from place to place. Money was not of this kind. It was a mere lubricant or a mere language. Money helped in the business of exchanging things wanted for their own sake, and it expressed the quantity of one good exchangeable for a given quantity of another in a language that made it easy to compare and to add up. Money played a part in exchange but did not seem to be of the essence of the matter. The theory of the essence of the business of exchanging things wanted for themselves was the theory of value. This left money unexplained. But why do we need explanations? We only want them if there are questions that trouble us. What were the questions about money? Some of them were these:

(1) Does money affect the mutual exchange ratios of other goods?

(2) Does money affect the sharing of the society's total produce?

(3) Does the level of money prices as a whole have any significance?

(4) Can money lift and lower the society's degree of productive activity as a whole?

It would no doubt be misleading to say that value was health and money was disease. But money seemed mainly interesting because of its power to upset things. A general rise of prices was troublesome for the paradoxical reason that it was not general enough. If some people were left behind in the misnamed general rise of prices, which includes the prices of people's work and other productive contributions, this might be unjust and might cause hardship. Besides, a general rise of prices seemed to call in question men's control of their affairs. Nobody in particular wanted a general rise of money prices, yet it could happen. And then, after all, money besides being a lubricant and a language was also a commodity. It was gold. Gold was the only British money that was ultimately acceptable to other countries. How was Britain to make sure of having enough gold? What caused gold to drain away, how could it be got back? There was much concern at various times about money. They were mainly the times when money seemed to have gone wrong and be causing trouble. There were theories of money which sought to explain the troubles and answer the questions. But since it was clear that if money could upset the business of exchange and the business of production, this meant that money was intimately involved in those businesses, there seemed to be a need for a theory which would embrace both value and money, which would unify them. Knut Wicksell in 1898, in his famous book *Interest and Prices*,[4] declared this need by his choice of title. For in its original German his book was called *Geldzins und Güterpreise*, and *Geldzins* of course means interest on money. Wicksell showed that money affects interest and interest affects prices.

Wicksell distinguished two meanings of the expression *rate of interest*. One of these was the percentage per annum at which business men could borrow money from a bank. The other was the percentage per annum which this money could be made to yield when employed in production and trade. The former was the money rate of interest, the latter was what he called the *natural rate*. If the money rate lay below the natural rate, it would pay to borrow money and use it to hire labour and buy materials and tools. Competitive bidding for these means of production would raise their money prices and, through this and through increases of quantity supplied, would raise the money incomes of their suppliers. The spending of these larger incomes on the very products in whose making they were earned would render production more profitable still, and engender a new round of competitive demand for factors. Thus the rises of price of factors and of products would continue their reciprocal process of enhancement so long as the money-rate of interest did not catch up with the natural rate. The cumulative process of price-rise, the inflationary process, sprang from and was sustained by the simple condition, that the cost per one hundred pounds of borrowed money should be less than the income derivable from the things that it would purchase. Wicksell had by this thesis taken three great strides. He had exhibited a mechanism for the influence of money on output as a whole, general productive activity. He had shown that the source of this influence was the readiness or the reluctance of banks to lend. And he had shown that the lever of this influence was an interest-rate, the money rate of interest by which the banks' readiness or reluctance was expressed. Wicksell did not, perhaps, envisage an increase of *quantities* of product per time-unit as an aspect of the cumulative process. He assumed, in conformity with the implications of value theory, that all available factors of production were always fully employed so that no actual increases of physical output were possible in the short period. The cumulative process was a price process. But its *mechanism* was an endeavour, on the part of each firm individually, to increase its physical output. If, instead of full employment, Wicksell had happened to envisage a starting point of heavy general unemployment, would he not have been obliged to infer that output would at first increase concomitantly with prices, or even instead of them? When Keynes took up the thread of Wicksell's thought, in the *Treatise on Money*, he hinted at the possibility that outputs, as well as prices, would respond to a relative lowness of interest-rates.

A lowness relative to what? Wicksell thought of the natural rate as being governed by the technology which was embodied in the existing stock of equipment, the stock of farms, forests, mines, machines and buildings, a stock whose size made possible a particular degree of division of labour, of specialisation amongst both men and instruments. Each addition to this stock would in principle make possible a somewhat better division of labour, but the efficacy of such an addition would be smaller the larger the stock to which it was added. Since the size of the stock could only increase slowly, it was the money rate which was the more volatile and easily changed of the two rates. The money rate was indeed changeable at the will of the banking system or the monetary authority, it was a policy instrument, its appropriate use would enable those authorities to prevent a general and continuing rise of prices.

By this suggestion Wicksell made possible a new stream of ideas. It is hardly too much to say that the macro-economics of today, at least in those freer forms which Keynes, in especial, would have given it, flows from the Wicksellian spring. For Böhm-Bawerk had drawn the rate of interest into the scheme of value-theory and encompassed it in the General Equilibrium system. He had bound it into the system of deliberate, voluntary, pre-reconciled and fully-informed actions by which all conduct can be explained as the response of reason to circumstance. Within such a system, there can be no involuntary acts, in particular, no involuntary unemployment. Wicksell remembered that interest is the price of a loan of money. But money does not belong to the value-system. It is created by the banks *ex nihilo*. To treat the interest on loans of money as the same thing, in nature, origin and governance, as the extra productivity of a more subtle division of labour, is gratuitous and baseless. The money rate and the natural rate are entirely distinct. And yet, as Wicksell himself pointed out, they must both be taken into one reckoning, for both are forms of income derivable from the possession of wealth.

If the money rate of interest is not a mere reflection of those influences which determine the rate of reward earned at the margin by the stock of capital equipment, then that reward is not the only incentive for income-disposers to leave a part of their money income unspent on consumption. But that reward will still be the sole inducement for businessmen to buy extra items to augment their capital equipment. The inducement to save, on one hand, and the inducement to invest, on the other, are divorced from each other in source and nature, and can thus be different from each other in numerical size. What, then, determines the money rate of interest?

The greatest innovation in Keynes's great trilogy of the *Treatise*, the *General Theory* and the epilogue in the *QJE*, is his theory of the rate of interest. It is presented in fullest freshness and liveliest colours, and almost in its completed form, in the *Treatise*. It does not emerge there all in one place and in one piece, but seems to take shape under our eyes in Keynes's thought. Discussion of it begins under the heading 'The price level of new investment goods', in the passage we have quoted in our chapter 2 from his pages 127 and 128, where he describes the two decisions facing the saver, namely, how much to save, and in what form to keep his savings. Here and throughout the *Treatise*, Keynes speaks of the alternatives of this second decision as 'savings deposits' and 'securities', meaning by the former simply money, and by the latter any and all of three things, namely, equipment, the equity shares which represent its ownership, or the bonds which acknowledge a borrower's debt. Sometimes he speaks of 'investments'. He says:

'It follows that the actual price level of investments is the resultant of the sentiment of the public and the behaviour of the banking system. The price level of investments as a whole, and hence of new investments, is that price level at which the desire of the public to hold savings deposits is equal to the amount of savings deposits which the banking system is willing and able to create. If we assume that banking habits and practices are unchanged, the requirements of the cash deposits [i.e. money held by individuals to meet their personal expenditure, and by business men to meet their business expenditure] are mainly determined by the magnitude of the earnings bill, i.e. by the product of the

rate of earnings and the volume of output; and the requirements of the saving deposits are mainly determined by the
bearishness of the public's disposition taken in conjunction
with the price level of securities. Or putting it the other way
round, given the total quantity of money, only those com-
binations of the rate of earnings, the volume of output and
the price level of securities are feasible which lead to the
aggregate requirements of money being equal to the given
total'. (pp. 128–32)

In these passages the key words are 'sentiment' and 'bearishness', and these will be our clue in tracing Keynes's path towards his completed doctrine.

We turn now to book IV of the *Treatise*, 'The dynamics of
the price level', where chapter 15 is called 'The industrial circulation and the financial circulation'. Some passages amount-
ing scarcely to a page in all give Keynes's essential account of
how liquidity preference, money supply and the interest rate
are bound together:

'The existence of savings deposits is an indication that there
are persons who prefer to keep their resources in the form
of claims on money of a liquid character realisable at short
notice. On the other hand, there is another class of persons
who borrow from the banks in order to finance a larger
holding of securities than they can carry with their own
resources. [Part of] the savings deposits comprise what, in
language borrowed from the Stock Exchange, we will call
the 'bear' position—including, however, as bears not only
those who have sold securities 'short', i.e. have sold securities which they do not own, but also those who would normally be holders of securities but prefer for the time being to
hold liquid claims on cash in the form of savings deposits. A
'bear', that is to say, is one who prefers at the moment to
avoid securities and lend cash, and correspondingly a 'bull'
is one who prefers to hold securities and borrow cash—the
former anticipating that securities will fall in cash value and
the latter that they will rise. Now when bullish sentiment

is on the increase, there will be a tendency for the savings deposits to fall. The amount of this fall will depend on how completely the rise in security prices relatively to the short-term rates of interest offsets the bullishness of sentiment. There will be a level of security prices which on the average of opinion just balances the bullishness, so that the volume of savings deposits is unchanged. And if security prices go still higher than this, then the volume of savings deposits will be actually increased. But the volume of savings deposits can only be maintained or increased in face of an increase of bullish sentiment, if the banking system deliberately brings about the rise in security prices by itself buying securities or if it takes advantage of the fact that differences of opinion exist between different sections of the public, so that, if one section is tempted by easy credit to borrow for the purpose of buying securities speculatively, security prices can be raised to a level at which another section of the public will prefer savings deposits. Thus the actual level of security prices is, as we have seen in chapter 10, the resultant of the degree of bullishness of opinion and of the behaviour of the banking system.' (pp. 223–4)

This passage contains in effect the whole theory of the interest rate to be found in the *Treatise* and the *General Theory*, as well as some highly condensed, elliptical and enigmatic sentences. We shall try to establish these claims and elucidate the puzzles.

The dominant impression which this passage makes is that of movement and change. Keynes is describing a game of wits, a scene of continual alteration of opinions, ownerships and circumstances, engendering and re-acting on each other. He is describing a *speculative* market, whose whole nature and mode of life consists in the holding of opposite views by two camps about what the impending price-movement will be, and in the attainment of a momentary stillness by means of an actual price-movement which transfers some members from one camp to the other. He speaks of 'a level of security prices which on the average of opinion just balances the bullishness', and then of '*differences* of opinion [his italics] between different sections of the public, so that if one section is tempted [to buy] securities speculatively, security prices can be raised to a level at which another section will prefer savings deposits'. These are two ways of expressing the same notion, of opinions about impending price movements being influenced (in ways which no statistical studies are likely to fasten into a stable function) by the movements which in fact ensue. The price which traces the play of a speculative market is inherently restless, its movements are in some degree self-generating. There is notably also the tacit but constant assumption that what is interesting is movement. Keynes discusses what will happen when 'bullish sentiment is *on the increase*' [my italics]. On page 225 of the *Treatise* he says:

'The total amount of the financial circulation [money serving as an asset or mediating the exchange of assets, rather than money mediating the process of production and consumption] depends, therefore, partly on the activity of transactions but mainly on the magnitude of the 'bear' position — both of these things being likely to be phenomena of rapidly *changing* prices rather than an absolutely high or low level.'

Why should this be so? What is the source of influence of 'changing' prices? Or rather, what is *meant* by 'changing' prices? Are they prices which *have* changed? But this in itself is irrelevant. All prices have changed, at some time or other in the past. Their existing level is an independent fact, whatever their past history. But are 'changing' prices, ones which are *going to change*? How do we know that they are going to? For anyone who feels that he does know, this impending change is of course vitally relevant. It is something he can take advantage of, by buying for a rise or selling for a fall. Changing prices must be ones which are *expected* to change because they *have just been changing*. The expression 'changing' prices is a telescoping of two intimately involved, but distinct, ideas. It is

puzzling to find Keynes making far less use of such words as
'expect' or 'anticipate' in the *Treatise* than Marshall had done
in his *Principles* [13] forty years earlier. Yet money is supremely
a vehicle for expectations. Its function and value are that it fills
a gap of knowledge, of what will be wanted and at what price
it will be obtainable at unspecifiable future times. Going back
to book III we find on page 143 a passage which illuminates
Keynes's tendency to an elliptical mode of thought on this
matter. In section V of chapter 11 he says:

> 'We have spoken so far as if entrepreneurs were influenced
> in their prospective arrangements entirely by reference to
> whether they are making a profit or a loss on their current
> output as they market it. ['are making' on their 'current'
> output? Does not this mean *have made* on their *immediate
> past* output?] In so far [he proceeds] as entrepreneurs are
> able at the beginning of a production period to forecast the
> demand for their product at the end of this period, it is ob-
> viously the anticipated profit or loss on new business, rather
> than the actual profit or loss on business just concluded,
> which influences them in deciding the scale on which to
> produce and the offers which it is worth while to make to
> factors of production. Strictly, therefore, we should say that
> it is the *anticipated* profit or loss [italics in the original]
> which is the mainspring of change, and that it is by causing
> anticipations of the appropriate kind that the banking sys-
> tem is able to influence the price level.'

Here, quite uncharacteristically, Keynes is willing to speak of
a period, and to envisage it as a period at whose threshold the
entrepreneur is momentarily placed. Yet, in the *Treatise*, the
spelling-out can be done naturally and easily, the shift to
expectational, ex ante language involves no contortion or re-
cantation. In the *General Theory* the divorce between essential meaning and explicit argument is far more troublesome.
For there we find identical equality treated as though it could
be a condition to be fulfilled, and we find those influences and
adaptive forces pointed out which can effect the adjustment.

It is, no doubt, an ellipsis rather than a fallacy. It was a piece of semantic sleight-of-hand which in the early days helped to give the *General Theory* its mystique. But, in so far as it depended on such false paradoxes, that mystique was somewhat illicit.

One more puzzle arises in the pages we quoted from chapter 15 of the *Treatise*. Keynes seems to assume that the banking system must always be an active participant in the events of the securities market. No doubt this is so if such events involve changes in the total quantity of money existing. But they need by no means do so. Security prices can change, the ownership of the securities can change, without any active role of the banking system and without any change in the total quantity of money. For it is apparent that the act of buying securities, otherwise than from the banks, does not abolish the money paid for them. The money and the securities are exchanged, both of them continue to exist. An increase of bullish sentiment can only cause 'savings deposits to fall' [in total quantity] if the bulls buy their extra securities from the banking system by drawing upon (and thus abolishing part of) their bank deposits or unused overdraft permission.

In discussing the prices of 'securities', Keynes is of course discussing interest-rates by implication. For securities include bonds, and a bond is the promise of a borrower to make a schedule of payments of stated amounts at stated dates. The percentage per time-unit at which the outstanding payments must be discounted in order to bring the total of their discounted values to equality with the price of the bond is an interest-rate. That price is the upshot of such market influences and movements as Keynes discusses. When it rises, the rate of discount calculated upon it falls, and vice versa. Keynes's ostensible concern in all of our quoted passages is with what governs the size of the total of savings deposits, but this concern itself is merely an aspect of his central problem, the source and governance of changes in the value of money. He finds it to be within the power of the banking system to determine that value, and its means of doing so is its control of the terms of lending, the market rate of interest:

'The only alteration which [the central currency authority of a country] has a power to order relates to the terms of lending. It is, therefore, via the alteration of the terms of lending that the change in the situation is initiated—this alteration affects the attractiveness of producing capital goods, which disturbs the rate [i.e. size of flow] of investment relatively to that of saving, which upsets the rate of profits for producers of consumption goods, thus causing entrepreneurs to modify the average level of their offers to the factors of production, and so finally achieving the ultimate objective of changing the level of money incomes. Thus—generally speaking—every change towards a new equilibrium price level is initiated by a departure of profits from zero; and this condition of equilibrium comes to the same thing as (1) the equality of saving and the value of investment, and (2) the equality of the "market rate" and the "natural rate" of interest.' (*Treatise*, p. 142)

This conclusion is the same at which Wicksell had arrived thirty years before. Theoretically at least, the banking system's lending rate, via its influence on other rates of interest, is the effective lever which lifts or lowers the number and the price of offers of employment, the size of the flow of output, and the general level of prices of consumption goods, the inverse of the purchasing power of money. Keynes well understood that the banking system's lending rate, a short-term rate, would have only a suggestive or trigger effect on long-term rates of interest. But we know in these days how vital a role can be played by ostensibly minute impulses, and this perhaps is even more dramatically true in human than in sub-atomic matters. But Keynes added a flood of extra light to Wicksell's searching ray—he brought in not only the speculative bond market 'determining', or tossing up and down, the long-term interest rate, but the notion of liquidity preference itself, which embraces the whole gamut of influences : speculative, political, diplomatic and even fashionable, which bear upon men's thoughts, emotions, imaginations and resolves. Keynes showed that interest is a *psychic* phenomenon, in a meaning wholly overshadowing simple time preference. The need to write the difficult *General Theory*, following the brilliantly lucid, seductively readable, confident and genial *Treatise*, was simply to bring the psychic and subjective origins of business action *in general* (not merely the rate of interest) from the outer darkness into the spotlighted centre of the stage. But psychic and subjective elements are not easy to make lucid, and the *General Theory* was a book even harder, by internal evidence, to write than to read.

The theme of the interest-rate, the questions what feature of the human phenomenon it reflects, what influences consequently bear upon its level and generate its changes, what in its turn it influences or governs and by what engenderment of opportunities and actions it takes effect, is as much present in the *Treatise* as in the *General Theory*, but in a different guise. The comparison of the two books in this regard is engrossing. Language is of importance here as elsewhere and may have its subtle influence on theory. In the index of the *General Theory* there are, under the headings of Liquidity, Liquidity-function, Liquidity-preference, Liquidity-premium, some fifty items. In the index of the *Treatise*, under Liquid and Liquidity, there are only four, and these refer only to capital or output, that is, to products and not to money. Since the *Treatise* discusses liquidity, need we be concerned as to whether or not it names it? There is a case for saying yes. The word liquidity draws together into a skein, a theme and ultimately a single idea the threads which, in the *Treatise*, tend to be separated by the classification of money holdings into two main and five subordinate kinds of deposit. Yet not even the *General Theory*, nor Sir John Hicks's 'Suggestion for Simplifying the Theory of Money', go the whole way. For money is needed only where there is uncertainty, and every need for it can be said to arise from the lack or impossibility of knowledge. The *Treatise* defines income deposits as money held 'to bridge the intervals of time between receipts and expenditure'. If a man were certain, at the moment of receipt of income, what needs were to be met out of that income, at what prices, there would be no need for any interval, he could buy, or at least choose and pay, at once. Money, in its role as the vehicle of consumption expenditure, makes it possible *for choice to be deferred until knowledge of needs and opportunities has improved* (i.e. has become more exact, complete or assured). Even the *General Theory* quite misses this idea:

> 'We can usefully employ the ancient distinction between the use of money for the transaction of current business and its use as a store of wealth. As regards the first of these two uses, it is obvious that up to a point it is worth while to sacrifice a certain amount of interest for the convenience of liquidity.' (p. 168)

But why is it *convenient* to have a store of *general purchasing power*? Because we are not yet sure what we want to buy. In so far as any money which a man is keeping in his pocket or his bank is being kept with a view to transactions, then it is being kept because of uncertainty; a petty rather than a momentous kind of uncertainty, if you wish, but for purposes of theory, of the *unity* of theory, this characterisation is important.

It is, of course, the 'store of value' aspect which is vital when we seek to explain why a person, or a business, should hold a stock of money. Keynes's passage on page 168 of the *Theory* continues:

> 'Given that the rate of interest is never negative, why should anyone prefer to hold his wealth in a form which yields little or no interest to holding it in a form which yields interest? There is a necessary condition failing which the existence of a liquidity-preference for money as a means of holding wealth could not exist. This necessary condition is the existence of *uncertainty* [Keynes's italics] as to the future of the rate of interest. If a need for liquid cash may arise before the expiry of [the n years of the term of a debt]

there is a risk of a loss being incurred in purchasing a long-term debt and subsequently turning it into cash, as compared with holding cash. There is, moreover, a further ground for liquidity preference which results from the existence of uncertainty, provided there is an organized market for dealing in debts. For different people will estimate the prospects differently and anyone who differs from the predominant opinion as expressed in market quotations may have a good reason for keeping liquid resources in order to profit, if he is right. [Keynes adds in a footnote to page 169] This is the same point as I discussed in my *Treatise on Money* under the designation of the two views and the 'bull-bear' position.'

Liquidity, then, is a *unifying* word. It reduces all the ostensibly distinct reasons for the use of money to a single reason: lack of knowledge; a lack remediable only at high cost or *logically*, *essentially*, *in the nature of things* not remediable at all. As economists we incur, I think, a legitimate charge of arrogance. We suppose men, even if only for the sake of argument, to know everything they need to know; or if not, we only concede that knowledge is expensive. After all the disasters of this century, is knowledge *still* only lacking because it is too expensive?

Liquidity is a term which seeks to bind into one idea all the reasons for holding ready money. So well does it succeed, that Keynes was impelled to write a special chapter which tries to dive down to the very foundations. In the famous or notorious chapter 17 of the *General Theory*, called by some 'mysterious' or by others 'pretentious', Keynes sought to show how liquidity preference works. For myself I believe that chapter 17 is not mysterious but only requires the reader to work out some meanings of symbols from what he is told about the formal frame where they appear. But I also think that in it, Keynes wholly fails to say *what liquidity is*. He talks, in that chapter, as though the meaning of the term is evident. In fact, however, he treats liquidity as an indefinable.

There are dangers in the unifying power of the term liquidity. For it may tempt us to assume (for practical expediency if not in basic belief) that liquidity-preference can be represented, for an individual, a firm or a society, by a stable function expressing the dependence of the interest-rate on the quantity of money. And in this regard we find the *Treatise* and the *General Theory* in sharp apparent conflict. The *Treatise* warns us as follows:

> 'If the volume of saving becomes unequal to the cost of new investment, or if the public disposition towards securities takes a turn, even for good reasons, in the bullish or bearish direction, then the fundamental price levels can depart from their equilibrium values without any change having occurred in the quantity of money or in the velocities of circulation. It is even conceivable that the cash deposits may remain the same, the savings deposits may remain the same, the velocities of circulation may remain the same, and the volume of output may remain the same; and yet the fundamental price levels may change. The degrees of change in the quantity of money, the velocities of circulation, and the volume of output will not be related in any definite or predictable ratio to the degree of change in the fundamental price levels.' (pp. 132–3)

Keynes uses the term bank rate to mean 'the effective rate which prevails in the market at any time for the borrowing and lending of money for short periods'. Bank rate is not rigidly linked with the total quantity of money. In the *Treatise* we read:

> 'Thus the total requirements of the monetary circulation are not associated in any stable or invariable manner either with the level of bank rate or with the level of prices; so that we shall be misled if we lay much stress on the changes in the total quantity of money when we are trying to trace the causation and the stages of transition. The order of events is not that a change of bank rate affects the price

level because, in order to make [it] effective the quantity of money has to be altered. A change in the quantity of money affects the price level in the first instance because this means a bank rate which will change the market rate of interest relatively to the natural rate.' (p. 197)

Such passages may be compared with the following in the *General Theory*:

'As a rule, we can suppose that the schedule of liquidity preference relating the quantity of money to the rate of interest is given by a smooth curve which shows the rate of interest falling as the quantity of money is increased. In the first place, as the rate of interest falls, more money will be absorbed by the transactions motive. In the second place, every fall in the rate of interest may increase the quantity of cash which certain individuals will wish to hold because their views as to the future of the rate of interest differ from the market views. It is interesting that the stability of the system and its sensitiveness to changes in the quantity of money should be so dependent on the existence of a variety of opinion about what is uncertain.' (pp. 217–18)

There are curious inconsistencies in the *General Theory* itself. We read:

'Experience indicates that the aggregate demand for money to satisfy the speculative-motive usually shows a continuous response to gradual changes in the rate of interest, i.e. there is a continuous curve relating changes in the demand for money to satisfy the speculative motive and changes in the rate of interest as given by changes in the price of bonds. Indeed, if it were not so, open market operations would be impracticable. In dealing with the speculative motive it is, however, important to distinguish between the changes in the rate of interest which are due to changes in the supply of money, and those which are primarily due to changes in expectation affecting the liquidity function itself. Open market operations may, indeed, influence the rate of interest through both channels; since they may not only change the volume of money, but may also give rise to changed expectations concerning the future policy of the Central Bank or of the Government. Changes in the liquidity function itself, due to a change in the news which causes revision of expectations, will often be discontinuous, and will, therefore, give rise to a corresponding discontinuity of change in the rate of interest.' (p. 197)

Is it fanciful to say that in the *Treatise* Keynes saw the lively play of a fish in the stream; that his attention was seized by its elusive dance and he resolved to examine it at close quarters; that in the *General Theory* he caught, named and dissected it; but that perhaps after all, the live impression that he gives us of liquidity preference in the *Treatise* brings us closer to the reality than his painstaking inspection of its dismembered carcase in the *General Theory*?

5. Keynesian Kaleidics

Keynes's work, in the *Treatise on Money* and the *General Theory*, was the means by which history itself was given important aspects of its shape during the past forty years. In that work he of course was giving intelligible form and expression to vast tides of inarticulate change which in no way took their origin from him. He was the interpreter. But he was by a huge margin the most influential of many writers who had insight into the nature and the source of events. He drew together strands of thought from several sources and showed them, at the end of his vast formulative and unifying effort, to reflect a single fact : that enterprise is a gamble and that the gamblers' nerve can fail, and that it is then open to them, in a money-using world, to sweep up their chips from the table and withdraw, leaving the real resources and means of production unemployed. This stark and simple message had to contend against the entrenched beliefs of Victorian optimism, left over from the half-century of comparative tranquillity that ended in 1914. Those beliefs recognized only reason, and supposed it to be paramount. Economic circumstance, in that view, rested at no great remove on the facts of the natural universe, and could accordingly be known, and being known, could be exploited by reason and the best advantage demonstrably gained from it. Keynes's task was to expose the fallacy in this view, to point out that human beings are an extra dimension of Nature, originative, ambitious, restless and insecure, that they do not know what they are next going to invent and to attempt, that reason is only a small part of the story. He himself began the *Treatise* with little inkling of what he would discover. The *Treatise* is confident, genial,

readable and clear. It is an eighteenth century book in its un-
hurried assurance. It appeals to past and contemporary history,
it shows the economic world to be a place where actions and
choices can be mistaken and can have unforeseen results, but
it does not declare that world to be a place where

> 'The practice of calmness and immobility, of certainty and
> security, suddenly breaks down. New fears and hopes will,
> without warning take charge of human conduct. The forces
> of disillusion may suddenly impose a new conventional
> basis of valuation. All these pretty, polite techniques, made
> for a well-panelled board-room and a nicely regulated mar-
> ket, are liable to collapse. At all times the vague panic fears
> and equally vague and unreasoned hopes are not really
> lulled and lie but a little way below the surface.'

From the ordered dissections in the *Treatise*, showing with
masterly succinctness and self-sufficiency how price-level
changes come about, to the nihilism of the article in the
Quarterly Journal of Economics [6] from which I have just
quoted, is a profound transformation. In undergoing this
transformation, Keynes's thought paralleled the course of real
events, the final dissolution of the stable and hopeful world,
the plunge from 1929, when the United States had discovered,
as was then said, 'the secret of permanent prosperity', to 1933
when the American national income in money terms had been
halved and even in real terms had been cut by a third, and
when Britain had sunk into unprecedented depths of depression and Germany had let in the Nazis.

The *Treatise* displays and makes explicit its debt to
Wicksell: [4]

> 'Wicksell's expressions can be interpreted in close accord
> with the Fundamental Equation of this treatise. For if we
> define Wicksell's natural rate of interest as the rate at which
> saving and the value of investment are in equilibrium, then
> it is true that, so long as the money rate of interest is held
> at such a level that the value of investment exceeds saving,

there will be a rise in the price level of output as a whole above its cost of production, which in turn will stimulate entrepreneurs to bid up the rates of earnings above their previous level, and this upward tendency will continue indefinitely so long as the supply of money continues to be such as to enable the money rate to be held below the natural rate as thus defined. Wicksell was the first writer to make clear that the influence of the rate of interest on the price level operates by its effect on the rate of investment. This increased investment causes an increased demand for actual goods for use, and it is this increased actual demand which sends up prices.'

Keynes refers to pages 82–84 of *Geldzins und Güterpreise* as his source for this argument.

Here, then, seems to have been the starting-point of the *Treatise on Money*. Wicksell was describing a situation of *disequilibrium*, a situation which must give rise to bodily shifts of demand schedules and thus of price levels, and a situation, moreover, which could be maintained in being despite these adjustment-seeking movements and thus cause them to re-generate the effects which gave rise to them and be themselves repeated indefinitely. It was the famous cumulative or self-reinforcing process. But we need not appeal to the nature of the Wicksellian spring from which the Keynesian insights flowed. The theory of the *Treatise* itself, as encapsulated in the Fundamental Equations, is a *disequilibrium* theory, a theory which visibly exhibits the active forces of change. And when we read the passage I have just quoted, in which Keynes condenses Wicksell to about 200 words, does not the thought irresistibly suggest itself : 'What more is there, regarding essential chains of causation, to say?'

What, in short, did Keynes need to add to the *Treatise* to make its argument complete? The answer to that question is itself suggested by inspection of the passages about Wicksell. What the *Treatise* comes down to, as the proximate cause of movement, the channel of all influences engendering it, is investment. And what the *Treatise* lacks is an adequate theory of investment. It was that which the *General Theory* had to supply, together with an expansion of the phrase 'an increased demand for actual goods for use' into a fully articulated Kahnian Multiplier. In both these questions the central enigma of Keynesian methodology appears. Why does the *General Theory* resort, in all formal analysis, only to equilibrium, to adjusted states of affairs, and eschew all such apparatus as the Fundamental Equations, which treat equilibrium merely as a special case?

The theory of the inducement to invest is a theory of the seeking of maximum gain. The natural form of such a theory is the equilibrium technique, the setting of a derivative equal to zero and the solving of the resulting equation for a value of the argument-variable. To suppose that the chooser of action uses this method is to suppose that he has all necessary knowledge, e.g. that in deciding on output he knows the shape of the demand curve facing his firm and likewise its cost conditions. Keynes faced a strange dilemma. His theory of employment or of output as a whole showed that a vital link in the chain of causation was investment. But this recognition by itself is hardly enough. What governs investment? He needed a theory of investment, both as a completion of his theory of employment and as an instrument of public policy, but the use he would make of a theory of investment, at the end of the day, would be to show that it was bogus. In the *General Theory* he propounded a gain-maximizing theory of investment on straight-forward marginal lines, a theory whose expressed form supposes the action-chooser to have all necessary knowledge. And in all the discussion which starts from this formal theory, his purpose is to expose that supposition as absurd and to draw the consequences of abandoning it. In chapter 12 of the *General Theory* he makes clear the non-existence (I would myself claim it to be a logical non-existence) of anything that can be called knowledge regarding the future years in which durable investment-goods must earn their cost and yield their gain. How can such seeming double-think make sense?

A detached examination of our discipline will show it to be full of indispensable double-think. Perfect competition, which is indispensable to the crowning achievement of the theory of value, its solving of the problem of the exact exhaustion of the product by payment of the factors at rates equal to their marginal productivities, is a remarkable example. Perfect competition is only realized when the number of suppliers, of a product amongst whose specimens all actual and potential demanders are indifferent, increases beyond all bounds as the size of every firm decreases. Such a firm can sell any quantity per time unit which it can produce, without any decline of unit price. Its total requirement of factors of production being negligible in proportion to the industry, it can attract extra quantities without offering higher pay. Yet if in given conditions of demand for its own and other products, the *industry* seeks to expand, it will of course have to reduce the price per unit of its product in order to compete with *other* products, and it will have to raise somewhat its offers of pay in order to draw off from the suppliers of those products some of their factors of production. The concept of perfect competition is protean, changing its meaning as our thought shifts from the firm to the industry or to the economy. If we are not exempt from double-think in one context, we cannot blame Keynes for resorting to it in another.

The economic theoretician is faced with insoluble problems of method. How can it be otherwise, when his subject-matter is the Human Affair which has baffled sages and scholars for ever? He has, in fact, been given to starting with answers and working back to questions, and I think this was inevitable. The answers were no doubt suggested by proximate questions: Why are some people rich and others poor? What accounts for the ratios in which things exchange for each other? How is it that men accumulate wealth? But these proximate questions lead to more fundamental ones. Economics has been called the pure logic of choice, but economists have not asked themselves what is choice? 'The pure logic of choice' is a phrase of doubtful self-consistency. If action is the upshot of the pure application of reason to adequately known circumstance, is it choice? It seems much like determinacy. Economics appears to have started with an answer: Men are reasonable and well-informed : and to have proceeded from this to the question: How does circumstance, both the minor 'accidents' of our private situation and the universal facts of Nature, shape our conduct and our institutions? But we could have asked a quite different question : Is men's conduct determinate? And if not, how can we understand it? The truth is that logic, however subtle and intricate, is certain and definite. Once we throw it off as the sole origin of conduct, we seem to have lost all bearings. The economic theoretician is impaled upon this dilemma. Do men act according to necessity, so that it is otiose to speak of choice; or are they masters of their fate, and if so, what is their guidance? His solution has been that he will have it both ways. He will not precisely be inconsistent at any one moment, in any one argument. But he will have a variety of pairs of spectacles, and use one or another according to that aspect of his immediate problem which most insistently presents itself.

Reason and choice is not the only pair of horns which confronts the economist. There is the business cycle. Is it genuinely a cycle, a unity whose phases all have, in effect, a single explanation, or is it merely a consequence of the ultimate restraints that the frame of things imposes on self-regenerating movements set going by random and various impulses? In the former case, how can the cyclical *mechanism* be reconciled with the supposedly rational governance of economic affairs? Do we opt for rational response to circumstance as our theory of history, or for subservience to the design of a machine? And there is money. It has no place in a purely rational system, for its two purposes are *search*, the finding of partners for multilateral exchange, and *liquidity*, a means of providing against contingencies; but rationality pre-supposes complete knowledge, which would abolish both these purposes. Is more illumination supplied by the value-theory model or the 'money-using' model? In face of such dilemmas, how can the economist hope to find an all-encompassing, exact and general model, simple enough to be intelligible to its own constructors? If he cannot do so, which requirements had he best give up?

Generalness of the model means here its capacity to embrace all aspects of the Scheme of Things, to allow all questions, which can be framed in terms of human experience of business life, to be put to it. They must be able to be put, not one at a time, but simultaneously. Since the world itself is a model, we cannot say that no model with these powers can exist. But it is because the world as it presents itself to us is not intelligible that we need a simplification. There seem to be two policies between which we can first choose. There is what I will call the tool-box policy. It consists in giving up the ambition of a model which would be general and comprehensive in the sense I have proposed, and being content instead with a variety of mutually exclusive models, each resting on assumptions some of which are rejected by the other models. This has been in fact the rather tacit and even unconscious policy of our profession. We have value-theory, which excludes the future; we have monetary theory, which is meaningless without the supposition that there is time to come; we have theories of cyclical recurrence according to some inherent design of human nature or institutions, which deny men the control of their affairs; we have expectational theories which, if they follow the logic where it leads, are bound to dissolve business affairs into a work of origination, a kind of pragmatic poetry; all these theories exclude each other's basic postulates and can only be used one at a time, like the hand-tools which an artisan takes up and lays down. Secondly, there is the policy of *imprecision*. There is the resort to the inner powers of language, the manifoldness of the meanings of words. Words can grasp lightly and delicately the meanings and essence of ideas, allowing those ideas as it were to move within the sentential frame and show different aspects to different hearers. This policy also has forced itself upon economists. Economics is an *essentially* imprecise subject. It treats collections of vast numbers of dissimilar things as scalar quantities : capital, a collection of things as naturally unlike as fields, flocks, looms, libraries and ships ; the general price-level, an average, arrived at by any formula we care to devise, of a list of prices composed in any way we can think of ; national income, the result, in principle, of pricing a million things and multiplying the prices by the quantities, all prices being ephemeral and being meaningful only 'at the margin'. Economics is the *art and science* of imprecision. It operates with capsules or 'black boxes', into whose contents we do not enquire. Or it treats of the central enigmas of our experience in terms of words so familiar that they banish misgivings and inhibit curiosity.

Within each of these two policies, the tool-box policy and the policy of imprecision, there is a second stage of choice. We can elect a theory which shows a state of rest or a system of tensions ; in other words, an equilibrium or a disequilibrium method. Equilibrium is one of the most powerful ideas of economic theory, equalled only, perhaps, by that of a system of inter-necessary activities, an organic system or Tableau Economique. Equilibrium has proved so incisive, general and unequivocal in providing insight that it dominates most of our theorizing. It is very hard to get away from, partly because of the prestige belonging to its nature, which is simply the supposition that men's conduct is governed by *effective reason*. But the equilibrium method itself shows how things would be if they were perfectly mutually adjusted, and says nothing about how they could become so. Instead, we can ask what will follow if such an equilibrium is in some sense and manner destroyed. In the end we have a fourfold classification : Equilibrium or disequilibrium within either the tool-box policy or the imprecision policy. And there is one more consideration. Whereas equilibrium is in essence unequivocal and unique, disequilibrium can be the source of endless different modes of thought.

If this classification or tree is a possible frame of reference, where in it does Keynes stand? By his own claim he wishes to be general. It is in somewhat the sense I have been giving to this word that the *General Theory* is general. We must not then expect him to be a tool-box theorist. The alternative is imprecision, or to give it a less seemingly pejorative name, the policy of reliance on the mysterious, subtle and fathomless powers of words. Finally, is he an equilibrium or a disequilibrium theoretician? In the *Treatise*, written from a background of practical experience in a vast arena, he saw the economic world as full of tidal forces and contending interests, a scene where disequilibrium must normally prevail. But in the *General Theory* he had discovered the need for an analytical tool. On the question what engenders and what governs investment, the *Treatise* is sketchy and casual. For a theory of investment we have in volume I a few succinct but scattered paragraphs, in volume II we have a reference to Schumpeter (as summarized by Wesley Mitchell) for fixed investment, and a paraphrase of the Austrian theory of capital for inventory investment. And are we to take it that the theory of investment was, in the *Treatise* days, only fit to be relegated to volume II? In the *General Theory*, the emphasis is different. There, not scattered paragraphs, but the whole of book IV, one hundred and twenty pages in a continuous tract, are devoted to The Inducement to Invest. And having recognized that the keystone of his arch was investment considered in its origin, nature and quantitative governance, Keynes went direct to the orthodox method, the marginal analysis. In the index of the *Treatise on Money*, the word marginal does not appear. In the index of the *General Theory* there are eleven headings under it. So Keynes was committed to the use of an analytical and a marginal technique for gaining insight into a matter where:

'The outstanding fact is the extreme precariousness of the basis of knowledge on which our estimates of prospective yield have to be made. Enterprise only pretends to itself to be mainly actuated by the statements in its own prospectus, however candid and sincere. If the animal spirits are

dimmed and the spontaneous optimism falters, leaving us to depend on nothing but a mathematical expectation, enterprise will fade and die—though fears of loss may have a basis no more reasonable than hopes of profit had before.'
(*General Theory*, pp. 149 and 161–2)

In order to have a name for the procedure which this extraordinary clash of method and meaning seems to impose, I have ventured in various places to call it *kaleidic*. When this word suggested itself to me, it was some thirty years since I had looked at the *Treatise on Money*. Forty years after that first reading (on 24 September 1972, when preparing these lectures) I was astonished to find the following sentence on page 81 of the volume in the Collected Writings:

'Nevertheless we must not argue that an expansion of the currency influences relative prices in the same way as the translation of the earth through space affects the relative position of the objects on its surface. The effect of moving a kaleidoscope on the coloured pieces of glass within is almost a better metaphor for the influence of monetary changes on price levels.'

If the economic theoretician is to organize his subject as a manifestation of human nature, and to trace it back to the operations of feeling and of thought, he must exhibit its events and situations as flowing from men's construction of their opportunities and their choice amongst those conceptions. In speaking of opportunities, the rival courses and associated sequels which confront the individual at all times, as things conceived or constructed, I am in the same breath appealing to reason and rejecting its claim to give unique, unequivocal guidance. Men in part *originate* their opportunities, using what suggestive materials the current of history carries fleetingly past their eyes. Men in large part set their own problems and try to work out the answers while there is yet time. In this activity they present two aspects to the observer. One aspect is the operation of reason and the exercise of preference amongst

its products. The other is the gathering of materials for reason
to use. Those materials will be partly common to all members
of the business society, partly special to different camps or individuals. And they will be continually altering in composition
and in the light which they throw on each other. If economic
theory is to be a theory of intelligent conduct in a flowing,
enigmatic and elusive world, both aspects must be embraced.
Keynes has hit upon a policy for this accommodation.

The *General Theory* shows us *reason* constantly proceeding
as if it had sufficient data, and being sometimes apparently
justified in this by the emergence of a general consonance of
assessments and intentions. These seeming states of general
adjustment, however, are to the last degree fragile and un-
stable, because their basis is inevitably at all times partly figment. Such a state of affairs, such a state of *ideas*, is we may
say a *haunted* equilibrium. Disillusion, once it occurs in any
part, can call everything in question. What follows such a
collapse must defy analysis, since reason for the time being
recognizes its own defeat and retreats into 'liquidity'. This also,
as Keynes continually reminds us, is, for the society as a whole,
merely another illusion. But it will lead to a new groping for
adjustment and eventually to a new equilibrium of this peculiar kind.

Such a method, if I am justified in discerning and naming
it as something distinct and coherent, has notable advantages
for practice. In the first place, it allows us to use our familiar
tools. Partial equilibrium expressed in pairs of curves, or in
families of indifference varieties with a budget constraint, can
still express the sought-after *good state of mind* for the individual in his capacity as supplier of productive services, income-
seeker and disposer, consumer and saver, or business man,
organizer, enterpriser and investor. What partial equilibrium
does for us is to show us reason at work, reason engaged in dis-
covering the implications of stated circumstances, whether
those circumstances have been able to be correctly observed or
whether (as when they consist in the future choices and
actions of other people) they are in their nature unobservable

and must be proxied by figments or conjectures. Reason *constructs* and then *interprets* circumstance. The curves and surfaces of our partial analysis cannot show the stage of construction, they exhibit the finished product of that stage. They show the demand-conditions which the business man assumes, on evidence strong or weak, and the cost-conditions which for remote years may be no easier to arrive at. After that, reason can proceed with its characteristic and prestigious assurance, telling what his output should be. When the question is what his investment should be, the philosophy and justification are the same, though the justifiable degree of assurance is far less, and as Keynes says in several places, is perhaps not relied upon at all. The angler makes his cast with all his skill, not knowing whether any fish will rise. The rewards of enterprise, those rewards which by the essential paradox of life are also incentives, are *imagined* gains.

Keynes's method (in so far as my gloss on it has any warrant) carries us a stage further. He considers how things will be in the productive society as a whole at those times when the explorations of 'partial equilibrists' contrive to coalesce into a seeming comprehensive adjustment. He describes the aggregative equilibrium with a supposedly given size of the flow of general investment. And it is of course investment which is the seat of practical trouble and of theoretical difficulty. The most conspicuous renunciation which the *General Theory* makes is in the absence from it, except in the sketchy and elliptical chapter 22, of any suggestion that changes of general output are an influence on the size of the flow of investment. Yet what influence more readily or more invincibly suggests itself? All the authors of business cycle theories which incorporate Keynesian elements have necessarily exploited this idea. Yet, despite the aberrant chapter 22, it must be said to go against the grain of Keynes's method. A business cycle theory describes a broadly regular progression from phase to phase, boom, downturn, slump, stagnation, recovery and boom. Keynes refers to such a progression in chapter 22. But he most conspicuously omits to offer any detailed and convincing account of the engenderment of each phase by the previous one. He says:

> 'The later stages of the boom are characterized by optimistic expectations as to the future yield of capital goods sufficient to offset their growing abundance and their rising cost of production [i.e. the rising cost of producing the capital goods themselves] and, probably, a rise in the rate of interest also. It is of the nature of organized investment markets, under the influence of purchasers largely ignorant of what they are buying and of speculators who are more concerned with forecasting the next shift of market sentiment than with a reasonable estimate of the future yield of capital assets that, when disillusion falls upon an over-optimistic and over-bought market, it should fall with sudden and even catastrophic force. Moreover, the dismay and uncertainty as to the future which accompanies a collapse in the marginal efficiency of capital naturally precipitates a sharp increase in liquidity preference—and hence a rise in the rate of interest. But the essence of the situation is to be found, nevertheless, in the collapse of the marginal efficiency of capital'. (p. 315)

This passage, it seems to me, elides any real account of the *origins* of the collapse of the schedule of the marginal efficiency of capital. And if Keynes was prepared to offer such an account, it ought to have occupied a central place in his theme, rather than figure in book VI called 'Short notes suggested by the general theory'. But in fact, the thesis of his general theory is that the marginal efficiency of capital, that confidence-borne vessel, can be sunk by hidden rocks and shoals of many different kinds, and that we have no good ground, in a theory which calls itself general, to single out any one such hazard for particular attention.

Let us come to the ultimate question : What was Keynes's theme of central meaning, and what was the demonstrative or suggestive formal scheme in which, taking his two nominally separate books in their essential and intricate unity, he came very near to presenting it? Let us first repudiate that arrogance in some of his expositors and critics, which has found parts of these books needless, negligible, beside the mark, even wrong in conception and argument. No parts of these books can be discarded as springing from a soil alien to that of the work in its essence and informing spirit. There is indeed the arched and buttressed body of the thesis, supporting everything and giving it shape, and upon this there hangs a garb of detail, of interpretation, of illustration and analogy, of historical evidence and vivid, live and stirring description of institutions and modes of conduct. Each of these components is indispensable to the total effect. Without the supporting and embellishing discourses, we should find the bare bones of the theory unable to speak to our experience, emotions and intuitions.

The two books are the same book. They express the same vision, the same distillation of experience, the same construction of thought. Yet their formal method and assignment of importance are vastly different. They do not form stages of a continuous evolution. The later book is by no means a clear-cut improvement on the earlier one, far from it. What the later book represents is the application of the apparatus of thought provided by the earlier book to a dramatically changed situation. The *Treatise* was published at the very moment when the western world was collapsing into apparent economic ruin, with national incomes halved in money terms and many millions unemployed. Keynes found himself in possession of a splendid diagnostic instrument, which only needed re-focussing, with a turn or two of its built-in means of adjustment, to bring before his eyes a revelation, resting on the human predicament itself, of the origin and nature of general business depression and breakdown of enterprise, with its necessary consequence of massive unemployment. The *Treatise* had to be re-written with this new purpose in view. Unfortunately, Keynes was seized with the idea of making it more conformable to academic modes of argument. He would not be content to march round the citadel of orthodoxy blowing his

trumpets and waiting for the walls to crumble. He would fight
on the enemy's own ground, with the enemy's own weapons.
Thus that beautiful epitome, the Fundamental Equation,
containing by implication, or able to allow with the easiest of
mental adjustments, everything we need for the task in hand,
was discarded. What the Fundamental Equation does is to
suggest questions. If profit is a consequence of divergence
between (intended) saving and (intended) investment, what
engenders such divergence? Whose action can give rise to such
divergence, and how, by what arithmetic and by what psychic
levers, does this action work? What conditions, what kinds of
circumstance, govern the effectiveness of that action? What
inherent possibilities of trouble reside in the two quantities,
intended investment and intended saving? The answering of
these questions, in whatever depth the economist feels to be
his business, will itself amount to the creation of a theory of
the general price level, general output, investment and employment. The key to all is investment. Investment, like the
engine of an aircraft, is the source of sustaining power and
therefore the most fatally vulnerable element. In the *Treatise*,
Keynes, unaware of impending disaster and the revelation of
that vulnerability, thought that all that was needed to keep the
flow of investment at a suitable level was appropriate action
by the banks. In the *Treatise*, there was still the picture of a
system that could be managed, by paying due attention to the
market's momentary thoughts and obsessions, so as to keep
everything going evenly and in good order. In the *General
Theory* that complacency was already in disarray. While still,
faute de mieux, climbing on the scaffolding of marginal efficiency of capital and the rate of interest, Keynes kept remind-
ing his reader and himself that the marginal efficiency of
capital was a fragile convention exposed to all the mutabilities
of thought; to the shifts of expectation fed on fragmentary,
confusing and randomly self-selected 'news'; that its foundations were in the minds of men who could lose their nerve
when they wearied of whistling in the dark.

Had Keynes held to the method of his Fundamental

Equations, had he seen it for what it is, the explicit contrasting of an outcome with the expectations which, in some interval of a real historic process, have partly engendered this outcome; had he expounded the equation in those terms as though presenting the accounts of an enterprise and explaining their origin in assessments and decisions made in the preceding months and years; he would have appealed instantly to the habits of thought of business men and made himself impregnable against the later assaults of his affronted colleagues. He would have been himself confronted with the essential questions which the first Fundamental Equation forces upon its beholder : What engenders investment and governs the size of its aggregate flow, what circumstance allows it to exceed or fall short of the concomitant intentions to save of the earning community including the investing enterprisers themselves and their firms, what circumstance tempts those enterprisers from time to time to be false to the spirit of their calling and makes it delusively seem possible for the society as a whole to accumulate wealth, to pile up the means of production, without choosing for those means some perfectly specific technological form which exposes them to all the hazards of obsolescence through future invention? Keynes, of course, in writing the *General Theory* did see precisely these questions and found their answers. What he did not do was to remember how the questions which he was answering had been expressed; how they had been expressed in the *Treatise* by himself.

The Fundamental Equations, of course, can express an aggregative equilibrium. It is the situation where $I' = S$ and where $I = I'$. It is an *expectational equilibrium*, a situation where for the moment the actions of individuals are harmonised despite a boundless diversity of assessments. It is an inherently precarious and even self-destructive equilibrium, whose mutually contradictory judgements will themselves be judged by events and many of them condemned. Those individual judgements themselves can be expressed, regardless of whether or not an aggregative equilibrium seems for the time being to prevail, in the forms of partial equilibrium. The individual investor can, should and will (given a little time for thought and decision) bring the marginal efficiency of his own investing activity to equality with the interest-rate which he must charge to those investments, if he adopts and adapts the notion of marginal efficiency as a suitable vessel for his ferment of thought, his bubbling and sparkling hopes and clouded powers of insight and penetration of the future.

All this can be seen as residing in the *potentiae* of Keynes's immense intellectual effort. He did not bring them to a perfect consummation. He relied perhaps too much on the policy of imprecision, expressed in his dictum 'forget about periods', his adoption of the time-blurring language of 'current' quantities, his hesitation over the difference of meaning and use between partial and aggregative equilibrium. He laid out on the bench the component parts of a *kaleidic* method. Some of the best such parts he discarded, some incompatible ones be included, the conception as a whole he left incompletely and awkwardly assembled. But he showed what economics can be in the hands of a man who combined in some degree the insights, the felicities and the inspired audacities of the mathematician, the historian and almost the poet.

References

1. Keynes, J. M., *A Treatise on Money*. London : Macmillan (first edition 1930, Collected Works edition 1971).

2. Keynes, J. M., *The General Theory of Employment, Interest and Money*. London : Macmillan (first edition 1936, Collected Works edition 1973).

3. *Economic Journal*, 47 (1937).

4. Wicksell, K., *Geldzins und Güterpreise*, 1898. Tr. as *Interest and Prices*. London : 1936.

5. Myrdal, G., *Monetary Equilibrium*. London : Hodge, 1939.

6. Keynes, J. M., The General Theory of Employment. *Quarterly Journal of Economics*, 51 (February 1937) 209—23.

7. Keynes, J. M., *A Treatise on Probability*. London : Macmillan, 1921.

8. Harrod, Sir Roy, *The Trade Cycle*. Oxford : Clarendon Press, 1936.

9. Samuelson P. A., A synthesis of the principle of acceleration and the multiplier. *Journal of Political Economy*, 47 (1939) 786—97.

10. Kaldor, N. A model of the trade cycle. *Economic Journal*, 50 (1940) 78—92.

11. Hicks, Sir John, *A Contribution to the Theory of the Trade Cycle*. Oxford : Clarendon Press, 1950.

12. Shackle, G. L. S., *Expectations, Investment and Income*. Oxford : Clarendon Press (first edition 1938 ; second edition, with an additional introductory chapter, 1968).

13. Marshall, A., *Principles of Economics*. London : Macmillan (first edition 1890, variorum edition 1961).

Index

Printed in Great Britain by
Western Printing Services Ltd, Bristol